Especially for

_____

From

_____

On This Date

_____

Heavenly

XOXO

for Women

Tender Tales and Inspiration to Warm Your Heart

BARBOUR
PUBLISHING

© 2011 by Barbour Publishing, Inc.

ISBN 978-1-61626-303-4

Cover and interior design: Thinkpen Design

Published by Barbour Publishing, Inc., P.O. Box 719, Uhrichsville, Ohio 44683, www.barbourbooks.com

Our mission is to publish and distribute inspirational products offering exceptional value and biblical encouragement to the masses.

 Member of the
Evangelical Christian
Publishers Association

Printed in the United States of America.

Contents

Introduction

Twenty-first-century women have their hands full! We rush from job to home, then back again—serving in a variety of capacities. At night, we tumble into bed, exhausted, our thoughts already on tomorrow's tasks. But take heart! There are blissful moments in the midst of all the chaos.

When we're walking with Christ, our spiritual eyes are opened to unexpected blessings in each day—a daughter's smile, a coworker's pat on the back, a husband's wink. An unexpected check in the mail, good news on the job, a note from an old friend. All of these are heavenly XOXOs— hugs and kisses. They usually come when we least expect them. . .but right when we need them. And what woman doesn't long for hugs and kisses? They provide the extra "oomph" we need to get through life's more complicated moments. We literally feel God's supernatural embrace. He cocoons us in His love, giving us strength from the inside out. And when night falls—either literally or symbolically—we can rest our heads against the pillow, knowing He's seen us through another day and will do the same tomorrow.

Oh, how God loves us! He whispers words of love in our ears during the quiet times and hollers them above the roar of the crowd when life gets noisy. His greatest desire is that we would understand the depth of His love and learn to love Him, too. Today, take a little time to watch for His XOXOs. Then, when you've caught one in hand, reach out and pass it along to a friend in need.

As Time
Goes By

Life is full of beauty. Notice it.
Notice the bumblebee, the small child,
and the smiling faces.
Smell the rain, and feel the wind.
Live your life to the fullest potential,
and fight for your dreams.

ASHLEY SMITH

Ah, how time flies! One day we're young—with girlish figures, trendy hairdos, and giddy crushes on boys. The next day we're sitting on the porch swing, reminiscing about days gone by and wondering why arthritis has set in. The years in between fly by, often eluding us. We miss the important moments, more focused on our schedule than God's little blessings. Our heavenly Father wants us to pay attention to the details, even when the clock is ticking, not just so we can remember "the good old days" but because He's sending us XOXOs by the hundreds. He doesn't want us to miss even one heavenly embrace. . .one "atta girl!"

What about you, daughter of God? Do you feel that life is fleeting? Rushing by all too fast? If so, then take a deep breath. Look around you. Ask for God's eyes to see beyond the norm. He wants to give you a peek into a world you've never known.

Do you see a sparrow lighting on a tree branch? Are you captivated by winter's snowfall or an evening sunset? Do the sparkling eyes of your child or grandchild bring a smile to your face? If so, commit that moment to memory. Close your eyes. Photograph it. Don't forget. For in that instance—before you even have time to draw a breath— God is giving you a gift unlike any you may ever receive again. This precious memory will someday feel like a warm embrace when it revisits you. And it will, you know. One day, all of the rush-about stuff will fade away, and you will finally see the things that really mattered—those beautiful XOXO moments. On that day, the memories will wash over you like a warm spring rain, making you feel young all over again.

But why wait? At every age—and every stage—we can count our blessings, naming each and every one as it comes our way. We can begin to see our lives as the gifts they are. In the here and now. Today. No, it's not always easy, especially when the woes of aging set in. Growing old isn't for sissies, it's true. Our joints may stiffen, our hair might grow thin, and certain body parts will surely decide to head south for the winter. But every day we're blessed to draw another breath is an opportunity to engage with God and with His children. So, take your eyes off of the clock. Quiet the ticking. Focus, instead, on the Lord, and on those He has placed around you. In other words, grab hold of today and embrace it as a thing of beauty.

*The fear of the L*ORD *is the beginning of wisdom,*
and knowledge of the Holy One is understanding.
For through wisdom your days will be many,
and years will be added to your life.

PROVERBS 9:10–11 NIV

Swing Away

By Martha Willey

I could hardly contain my excitement as we pulled into my sister's driveway.

"Tell me again what Aunt Susan said to you when she called this morning," my daughter Carol asked as she turned off the car engine.

"She told me she had a time machine and that I should come right over and see it," I said.

"Oh," Carol said thoughtfully.

"I know your aunt can seem a bit strange now and then, but she sounded just fine this morning."

"You don't think talking about a time machine is strange, Mother?"

Actually I had found it a bit odd, even for Susan. My sister had slowly been developing holes in her thinking, but I wasn't as bothered by these lapses of time or the crazy notions Susan came up with as the rest of my family was. I would just respond to whatever place and time Susan thought she was in.

My daughter wouldn't have known anything about Susan's claim of a time machine had I not needed her to drive me to Susan's house. Carol, along with my son Chet, sat me down a week ago and told me the time had come to hand over my car keys. "You're almost eighty-five, Mother, and with the recent accidents you've had, we feel it's time for you to stop driving and let us take you where you need to go," Carol said.

I objected, of course. "All I hit was the mailbox."

"And the neighbor's car," Carol said.

"You ran into your own garage, Mother," Chet said.

I could not convince them otherwise, so now I was at the mercy of their schedule and their comments about visiting my sister who was slowly slipping away into a world of her own making.

Carol's next comment brought my thoughts back to the time at hand. "I just know that when I talked to Becky yesterday she said her mother was having a bad day. Aunt Susan stood at the front door all day waiting for Uncle Romer to come home from work. How could she forget that her own husband died ten years ago? Becky was beside herself."

"Becky's always beside herself." I loved Susan's daughter, Becky, but she could be a bit high-strung. "Becky needs to do what God says—worry less, trust more."

"I just don't want you getting upset if Aunt Susan isn't herself today," Carol said.

"I'm not an easily crushed flower, Carol," I snapped. When I saw her hurt expression, I felt a stab of regret. "God will give me the strength to face whatever mood Susan's in. I'll be fine, honey, really. Now please help me out of the car."

In a few minutes my niece Becky was letting us into the farmhouse she and my sister shared.

"Mother's out back with her time machine," Becky said smiling.

"Not you, too." Carol groaned shaking her head.

"Come on, Aunt June. I'll help you out to the backyard," Becky offered.

"I can find my own way," I said, pushing my walker along in front of me. I came to the back door of the house and looked out. There sat my older sister Susan on a porch swing. I couldn't believe that with her bad hip she was able to swing.

She greeted me with a huge smile. "Oh June, you're here. Isn't this just wonderful? Becky bought it for me as an early birthday present."

The swing was made out of white wicker. The thick seat cushions were covered with a bird-print material that was soft to the touch and beautiful.

"Sit down and take a load off," Susan said with a smile.

I eased my body down. My behind had barely touched the cushion when she pushed us off. "Isn't this grand?" she asked.

I looked at where the swing was attached to the ceiling. "Are you sure this is thing is safe?"

"Very. My son-in-law super-reinforced it. Stop worrying. Isn't this fun?"

A soft breeze caressed my face. My niece's flower beds were an array of colors—red, orange, yellow, and white. Yellow finches fed at one of the many bird feeders in the yard. A wind chime gently jingled nearby. I felt myself relaxing. "You know, I can't remember the last time I sat on a swing," I said.

"This isn't a swing. . .it's a time machine," Susan said.

I looked at my sister, and tears stung my eyes. I resolved to stay strong. I played along. "And where are we going to be traveling to?" I asked.

Susan laughed. "I've got both oars in the water, June, at least at this moment. I know we're sitting in a swing. But it's also a time machine."

"What do you mean?"

"Do you remember our old swing set? How the ropes cut into our hands?"

My mind cycled back through the years, and soon the memory of my swing set became clear. The seats were wooden boards painted red and the metal poles were bright blue. How I loved swinging, pumping my legs as fast as I could, my ponytail bouncing back and forth in the breeze.

"Yes, I remember. I haven't thought about that swing set in years."

Susan smiled. "We used to get so high up in those swings that we could see all the way to the Nichols' dairy farm over a block away."

"Mom caught us one time, remember? She came running out of the house and yelled at us to never swing that high again."

"She was always afraid the ropes would break and we'd go sailing off into space," Susan said. "Did I ever tell you I once caught Mom outside on my swing?"

I looked at my sister, shocked. "No. Really? Mom was swinging?" I just couldn't imagine my mother sitting on a swing. She would always push us, but she refused to swing herself.

"She was up every bit as high as we used to go."

I smiled at the image of my prim and proper mother swinging. "What did she say?"

"She said only adults were allowed that high, not twelve-year-old girls."

"Just wait until I join her in heaven one day. I'm going to remind her of her double standard." I laughed.

We lapsed into silence for a few minutes, just enjoying the whooshing sound of the swing going back and forth.

"Do you remember any of the things we talked about while we were swinging?" Susan asked.

I chuckled. "Do you know how many years back you're asking me to go?"

"Come on. One memory."

"Well, okay. We used to talk about what we were going to be when we grew up. You were going to be a famous painter with your artwork hung up in museums all over the world."

"You were going to be a princess and a librarian." Susan giggled.

"I got one out of the two. Do you regret that you never got to go to art school?"

Susan married right out of high school because her boyfriend was being sent to France to fight in the war. She found work in a factory; then when he returned they started raising their family. The only time she picked up a paintbrush after that was when she was painting her children's bedrooms.

"Now and then, but God helped me make peace with that a long time ago. Besides, can you imagine me in college? You know what kind of student I was."

"The one voted most likely to think of trouble, cause trouble, and be in trouble."

"You weren't always an angel yourself," she reminded me, as she gave the swing a push.

"True," I admitted. "I wonder what ever became of Mr. Stillman."

"The teacher who looked like Cary Grant?"

"I was *so* in love with him." I swooned and I felt my face grow red as Susan stared at me.

"I didn't know that. You never told me."

"You would have laughed."

"Probably. But I wouldn't have laughed for very long. You know, I saw him the other day at the pharmacy. He said he has to take about a dozen pills to keep his body going."

"I suppose he's fat and flabby."

"Who?"

"Mr. Stillman."

"Were we talking about him?" Susan asked, as the swing slowed down.

"Yes." I gave the swing another push.

"Just now? I. . .ah. . .don't remember." She looked so troubled I reached over and patted her hand. "I hate it when my mind fails me." Tears sparkled in her eyes.

"It's okay, dear." I handed her a tissue from my purse. "Let's switch to someone more interesting. Billy Harsher." I hoped Susan would remember him. All the girls at our school had a crush on Billy Harsher. He was like a Ken doll, perfect in every way and always with a smile on his face.

Susan beamed. "Who could forget him? Remember how we used to sit on our swings and call ourselves Mrs. Billy Harsher?"

I nodded. "When we were swinging we never had to worry about Mom and Dad overhearing us talking about the cute boys at school."

"They would have had a fit if they knew how boy crazy we were." Susan laughed.

"Remember the time you jumped out of the swing and

broke your foot?"

"That was bad." Susan nodded.

"Bad? You got to lie around eating ice cream while I had to do all your chores."

"Yes, but I couldn't swing. I felt like I was a bird whose wings had been clipped."

She still sounded sad over missing time out on her swing. I gave her arm a squeeze. "What else do you remember?"

"The concerts we gave."

I burst out laughing. We used to sing hymns at the top of our lungs while we swung. "It's a wonder no one ever called the cops on us for disturbing the peace."

"Remember the time we tried to paint our fingernails while we were swinging?"

"Or that time the fly flew in your mouth?"

We went back and forth reminding each other of all the conversations that took place while we were swinging. After a while we turned from the past to the present. I told her how much I hated not having my car.

Susan told me that Becky was going to quit her job because she didn't want Susan home by herself. "She says she doesn't mind, that this gives her a chance to do for me after all the years I used to do for her."

"Carol's said the same thing to me. It's still strange, though, don't you think? To have our children waiting on us?"

Susan nodded. "When God said He would meet my

needs I never thought it would be through my children."

We lapsed into silence then, weighted down by thoughts of our aging and the limitations it put on us.

Suddenly I grabbed Susan's hand. "What is it?" she gasped. "Did you throw your hip out?"

"No. I was just thinking that when Dad put those swings up, we were too little to get them going. We needed him or Mom to give us a push."

"So?"

"If we hadn't let them help us, we would have been stuck. Accepting an offer of an extended hand isn't a bad thing, and you know I don't exactly mind not having to smile for a driver's license photo. I always looked like a hoodlum."

Susan considered this. "Hmm, it *is* kind of nice not having to figure out what to cook for dinner."

"No paying for gas!" I joyously shouted.

"No dusting!" Susan giggled.

"No having to do laundry."

"No Raisin Bran."

I stared at Susan. "What?"

"I get to eat the same marshmallow sweet stuff the grandkids eat."

"With no car insurance to pay for, I can afford to buy material for the quilt I've always said I was going to make."

"And I can get the puppy I never could have when I was

living in my apartment."

"Perhaps our current life changes aren't too awful after all," I admitted.

"We've been really blessed when you consider our eighty-some years of life," Susan mused.

"God has faithfully provided for us just like He promised He would."

"Definitely. I may forget Him, but I know He won't forget me," Susan said.

I gave her a quick hug.

Becky stuck her head outside the back door, "If you two 'swingers' are done, lunch is ready."

"Coming," Susan said. We let the swing stop.

"We've had some of our best times on a swing, haven't we?" I said.

"It's where I learned I could come to you about anything."

"It's where I learned you would be there if I needed you," I said. "I never realized how sitting on a swing would bring back so many wonderful memories. You were right to call this a time machine."

Susan smiled. "You know one of the nicest things about a time machine swing is you can get on board for a ride any time." She and I looked at each other and began pumping our legs as fast as our arthritis would allow.

"I don't think a few more minutes of time travel will hurt," I said, grinning.

Susan smiled. "Swing away, sister, swing away."

A Better Story

The spiritual life is a life in which
we wait, actively present to the
moment, trusting that new things
will happen to us, new things that
are far beyond our own imagination,
fantasy, or prediction. That, indeed,
is a very radical stance toward life
in a world preoccupied with control.

Henri J. M. Nouwen

Have you ever paused to think about the script of your life? Who's writing it? Most twenty-first-century women would give themselves the credit, wouldn't they? But there's only one Author, and He's in control of our life-script. He alone knows where the plotline is headed—up, down, or otherwise. And we've got to trust Him at every step along the way. Sure, we've got great plans for tomorrow. Possibilities abound, and we want to make the most of every opportunity! We like to know where we're headed and how we're going to get there. But at some point we've got to admit that we're not the ones in control. God is. And He can—and should—be trusted.

Trust isn't easy, particularly when life's circumstances are gloomy. And when we're in a real mess—say, financial troubles set in, or we face an unexpected tragedy—handing over the reins can be more difficult than ever. Oh, but we serve a God who loves us! Pause to think about that for a moment. He created us! He breathed life into our very being. Was there in the delivery room when we were born. Walked us through the ups and downs of childhood. Saw us through those tumultuous teen years. He saved us by sending His only Son. Gave us new life in Him. Put us on a straight path. How, then, can we not trust Him with our life-script? He's the very One who's been penning it all along.

If you're at a point in your life story where you feel stuck, maybe it's time to drop the pen. Hand it to the real Author.

And look around you! You'll find others doing exactly the same thing. One by one, God's kids are coming to grips with the fact that they're not very good scriptwriters. They're relinquishing control, placing it into His capable hands. Imagine what an incredible place it would be if we all simply placed our trust in Him.

As that pen slips from your hand to God's, watch for heavenly embraces. They will alleviate your fear and give you courage to trust, even when you can't see what's coming around the bend. And remember, the Lord's plans for you are far greater than any you could have come up with. In other words, He's writing things into your script that you would never have thought of! Things far beyond the imagination.

So, brace yourself! Amazing adventures are coming. Surprises loom just over the horizon! Watch for those XOXO moments. . .those hugs and kisses from on high. They will serve as reminders that taking your hands off was exactly what God wanted you to do all along and will invigorate you to keep on keepin' on. In the meantime. . .trust, sister. Trust.

He is the image of the invisible God,
the firstborn of all creation.
For by him all things were created,
in heaven and on earth, visible and invisible,
whether thrones or dominions or rulers or authorities—
all things were created through him and for him.
And he is before all things,
and in him all things hold together.

COLOSSIANS 1:15–17 ESV

The Sign of the Pink Flamingo

BY VALORIE QUESENBERRY

Ellen peeked around the corner of the house and chuckled. It was perfect. And what a beautiful day for her little scheme—sunny as usual in northern Florida, but one of those days that had a tang of citrus in the air and a glint of gold in the sky. Not too hot. Made you glad you had given the coats to Goodwill, tossed the snow shovel in the dump, and embraced life in paradise.

Yeah, she had been hesitant when Richie announced his desire to be a permanent snowbird. But, land's sake, she wasn't one of those girls who couldn't admit to being wrong once in a while. And being down here gave them a good excuse to take a few road trips each year to see the grandkids. And how she and Rich loved to ramble! My, they had always been a pair of globe-trotters.

Ellen pulled the steaks out of the fridge and set about mixing up the marinade. None of those envelope mixes for her. A little vinegar, some olive oil, a dash of Worcestershire, and some sprinkles of several different spices and watch out, Food Channel! Ellen's steaks were legendary in the family.

Now, back to the musings. . . Oh sure, the trips they made. Well, back in the day, the Hartons were quite the family for taking that annual vacation; and after the kids left home, she and Richie had seen no reason to curtail their traveling penchant. Oh, the miles they had logged on that old Dodge. In her mind's eye, Ellen could see it now, plowing down the highway, she and Rich with the windows rolled down, a couple cans of soda in the console and the open road ahead of them.

"That's the way to adventure!" Richie always said of a morning. It was his way of starting the day, telling her that he was ready to hit it hard again.

Putting the steaks in the fridge, Ellen leaned down and lifted the foil on the dessert. Yes, it was setting nicely. Jell-O cake was another of her specialties. She imagined Rich getting ready to enjoy a large slab, slathered in whipped topping. He had a way of smoothing out the whipped cream on top with his fork before he took the first bite. It was a kind of ritual.

Ellen sat down to take a breather. It wasn't all it was cracked up to be, this getting older. She risked a look at her ankles and shook her head. How did they have the nerve to get puffy like that? Ellen Billings Harton had always had the slimmest, most delicate ankles of the bunch. Well, that's what Richie always said. Just like him to say something like that, too. He wasn't like other men, her Rich. He had a knack for noticing the unusual, the small, the ordinary. And she loved him for it.

That's why she was sure she had made a good choice. Oh, that man had better come home on time from his fishing trip today. . . .

* * *

"What happens now?"

Noel slapped her palms on the desk and sighed. It was always the same. You get to a point in the story and the ends begin to unravel. How to keep it together? Should it be happy or sad? Tragic or triumphant? Maybe Richie will die on his fishing trip, and Ellen will plant the pink flamingo at his grave as an eclectic reminder of their love. What if Ellen is really a nursing home resident with Alzheimer's disease and this story is taking place in her mind and she dies to be reunited with Richie? Maybe it should be a bland, fluffy story where Richie comes home, Ellen burns the steaks, and they all live happily ever after, chortling about their horrid pink flamingo in the front yard. And why a flamingo anyway? Noel shook her head; she hated those awkward-looking birds. Why had she chosen that as an icon of lasting love?

A drive. . .she needed to get out of the house. Sure, it was ten below and snowing furiously. That's why she had set the story in Florida. For goodness' sake, a writer did have the luxury of imagination.

Alaska was a land of wonders, to be sure. Every time Noel set her foot outside the door, she wondered how any living creature survived here—darkness for weeks at a time and the bone-gripping cold that clenched this primal, fascinating wilderness.

She unplugged the contraption that kept her car battery from freezing and started the engine. *Thank you, Daddy, for making me buy a good car.*

Backing out of the garage, Noel headed to Walmart. Always open; good American enterprise that they were. She needed a few things anyway—batteries and maybe some orange juice. All that writing about Florida made something citrus sound good.

The highway department was doing their job. The parking lot was doable. Of course, most of the people who lived here could drive in a blizzard blindfolded. It came with the lifestyle. There was a code of stoutheartedness around here. The people, quite simply, were amazing. And, as yet, Noel hadn't made it into the club.

She was thankful for her boots on the tramp into the store. And, oh, wonderful heat blowers that blasted with gale force as you stepped into the outer entrance. Just like an enormous blower dryer. What a wonderful man who invented that little gadget!

"Hi, Harry!"

Noel smiled to the greeter. He was her favorite. They all knew her, though—the lonely, crazy girl from the Lower 48 who was always dashing into the store for just a couple items. Why couldn't she shop all at one time like a normal person? She hadn't figured out what kind of disorder it was, but since her mother and sister did the same, it must be incurable.

Harry smiled back. "Hi, Miss Noel. Did you forget something?" He winked.

"Batteries. And I need some orange juice."

"I heard that. You better keep up on your vitamin C. My wife says it will keep you from catching cold."

"Absolutely! I'm going to do that." Noel waved and turned toward the chilled foods. *Pick up the juice and then grab a pack of batteries close to the checkout counters.*

While she walked, she pondered the plot of her story. There had to be a perfect ending. How could she surprise the reader?

Stopping in front of the juice compartment, she noticed how many of the cartons proudly proclaimed "Florida Orange Juice." It was like a seal of excellence. Okay, she had to work orange juice into the story line. Maybe Richie could buy a grove of oranges or Ellen could be drinking orange juice in the nursing home as she remembered.

Good grief, this is getting bad. Maybe she'd better just trash the whole story.

"Excuse me, do you know if this brand is any good?"

Noel looked up and then looked farther up. The guy was tall and was holding out a carton of orange juice, a question in his eye. But it wasn't the juice that made her stammer. It was what was under his arm. A long-legged, blushing pink, metal flamingo.

She almost giggled.

"Pardon?"

"I know this sounds crazy, but I can't remember which kind of orange juice my mom buys. Do you know what's good?"

"Not crazy. I love good orange juice." Noel held out the carton in her own hand. "This is what I always get, and it's pretty decent. Not quite like fresh-squeezed, but a fair imitation."

"Great." The guy picked up an identical carton. "I really appreciate this. I'm fixing breakfast in the morning." He grimaced.

Noel knew it was bad manners but said it anyway. "Your wife must really appreciate that."

He met her gaze. "Not my wife, my colleagues. We're from Florida, here on a fishing expedition and taking turns with the meals."

Noel felt foolish. Justifiably so. "Oh." That was that.

She took a step away. "Well, I hope your breakfast turns out well." She was dying to know about the flamingo, but there was no way she was going to stick her neck out twice. The first chop hadn't felt that good.

"Thanks." He turned also. "Hey, wait a minute. There's something else."

Noel swung around.

"I need an honest opinion. Do you like flamingoes?"

No way. A complete stranger asking about. . .flamingoes? "Well, they've never been my favorite bird, but. . ." Noel searched for a way to get out of this tactfully. *Okay, you're a writer; words are your thing. Think!*

He smiled. "Perfect. You said exactly the right thing."

"I did?"

He stuck out his hand. "I'm Richie."

She was going to faint in the juice aisle. "Richie? Are you sure?"

Now he stared at her. "Yeah, last time I checked, it was my name." He grinned. "Is that unusual?"

Just tell him the truth, stupid as it sounds. "You're not going to believe this, but. . ."

He was looking at her with clear blue eyes. Yeah, they were nice. Too bad. She was going to destroy the whole thing right here.

"You see, I'm a writer. And right now, tonight in fact, I'm working on a story called 'The Sign of the Pink Flamingo,' and one of the character's names is Richie, and they live in Florida, and he goes fishing. So, when I saw that flamingo and heard your name, well that's why I. . ."

He laughed. Really laughed. It was deep and nice. And

she laughed with him. What else can you do when you meet a good-looking man in the orange juice section who has a pink flamingo under his arm and smiles when you really botch an introduction?

He shifted the juice in his hand and smiled. "I'm really flattered. And I hope it's a best-selling story."

"Me, too. It probably won't be, though, unless I can think of a decent ending. That's why I'm here. . .to think."

"You think in Walmart?" It was gentle humor.

Noel looked at the ground. "Yeah, a little weird, but lots of times, it works."

"Hey, whatever works, I say. Look. . .I've got a confession. I don't really need orange juice."

"Huh?" Gifted writer she was, Noel couldn't make the connection.

"I am cooking breakfast in the morning, but none of us drinks orange juice. It was the only thing I could come up with to meet you."

"I don't understand." But Noel's heart was starting to do the staccato thing.

"I saw you walk in and overheard what you said to the greeter about orange juice. Figured it was as good a place as any to meet you."

"You wanted to meet me?"

"Very much. I've got another confession to make. I've been stalking you."

"What?"

He raised his hand in defense. "I mean, I noticed you in the church I visited last Sunday and well, I'd love to get better acquainted. How about a cup of coffee and a talk?"

Now the heartbeat was definitely intensified and her face felt warm to boot. But for all that internal action, Noel's tongue was helpless. What does one say at a time like this? What would one of her characters say?

It just popped out. "Richie, do you like road trips?"

He looked puzzled.

"How about slim ankles and steaks with special marinade?"

"I'm not sure I follow the line of thought, but it sounds great to me."

It was her turn to grin. "Yeah, I think Ellen would approve."

"Excuse me?"

"I'll tell you later. And I would love to have coffee. But first, I have to pick up some batteries before I check out."

He pointed into his cart. "I already got 'em. Thought it would save time."

Noel felt a certain kinship to Ellen. Some things must go with the name. He did seem like a Richie.

"Thanks. I guess we can go straight to the checkout then."

"I'm on the way." He stopped suddenly. "Hey, you still haven't told me your name."

"It's Noel. I'm surprised you didn't know it," she teased.

He grinned. "Tried to find out, but couldn't." He stopped in front of the checkout line. "So, shall we go across the street for some coffee now?"

"I'd love to. But first, I have to know, why are you buying a flamingo?"

He stopped the cart and looked at her. "Funny you should ask. Blame that on my grandmother. She said it was important that the right girl for me be honest, and she was crazy about flamingoes—said they were an unknown symbol of undying love. I guess I knew if you would be honest about not liking flamingoes. . .well, let's just say it was my moment of truth. And you know, this pink bird is kind of growing on me. . . ."

Noel just smiled. She knew just how she was going to end that story. Tonight, after she enjoyed a cup of coffee with this fascinating man who just might be the one to take road trips to the grandkids with her someday, she'd finish the manuscript and send it off.

"Richie?"

"Yes?"

"Have you ever eaten Jell-O cake?"

In Good
Times
and in Bad

When we worship the Lord,
let's remember that He is in control.
Nothing alarms Him, or takes Him by
surprise. Nothing is too big for Him
to handle, or so small it escapes His
attention. When the winds of my world
begin to blow, He remains seated.
When raging waves surround me,
He governs their temper. . . .
I need not be moved.

RONALD JAMES

Life can get overwhelming at times. Problems seem to rush at us from every side, and we feel weak. . .worn down. Exhausted, even. And just about the time we think we can draw a clean breath, here comes another disaster. Will we ever catch a break?

Because we live in a fallen world, things aren't perfect (much as we'd like them to be). Things don't always go as planned. For the believer, though, there is hope. God can take those things—good, bad, and ugly—and turn them into a thing of beauty. We don't have to let the chaos of life wear us down. We can be triumphant, even in our weakness.

It's hard to imagine sometimes, to be sure. This is especially true when our defenses are down or when we're genuinely wounded. There are events so catastrophic that we can't envision God ever using for good. But if we're watching closely, we will see that He's trying to do just that. If you could see beyond the hovering clouds, you would notice glimpses of sunlight peeking through.

Likely, you don't care to see the rays of sun. Not when you're upset. But how else will you ever find healing? If you're in a fist-shaking season—things have been really rough—unclench those fingers. Take a deep breath. Look around you. What do you see? The stars still twinkle at night. The grass is still green and lush in the daytime. Mothers are still singing lullabies to their children. Folks still drive by in cars and trucks, headed to work or play.

In other words, the world doesn't stop spinning, even when it feels like it should. Life—with all of its fair and unfair moments—goes on, whether you want it to or not. And what you do with that life can make all the difference. You can strong-arm it, disgusted with the circumstances you've had to walk through, or you can embrace it, arms wide open. Remember, God's strength is made perfect in us, and there's no better time to experience that than when we're at our weakest.

So, why not make this an "arms wide open" day? Even if you've been through something tragic. *Particularly* if you've been through something tragic. And praise God, even if you don't feel like it. Open that mouth and let the praises ring out! What the enemy meant for evil in your life, God can—and will—use for good. But you have to let Him. He wants to touch you. To heal you. To wrap you in His arms for some XOXO time. So, take a few steps in His direction today, even if it's difficult. Deep breath. Healing is on its way. Just believe.

I will bless the Lord at all times:
his praise shall continually be in my mouth.

PSALM 34:1 KJV

Two Strong Legs

SHERRY'S STORY (AS TOLD TO AMY BLAKE)

I helped my three-year-old son into the car, set my Bible on the seat, and closed the door. Shading my eyes with one hand, I watched my husband hoe our garden. His strong body battled the weeds crowding our plants, and his determined face made it clear he would win the fight.

I steeled myself and called, "Terry, we're heading for church now."

He stopped work and stomped across the grass toward me. I cringed, seeing in his face the anger only my new-found faith provoked.

Before he could start hollering, I worked up enough nerve to ask, "Do you want to go with us this time?"

His face reddened, and he ripped off his work gloves. "How many times do I have to tell you, Sherry? I don't need your religious crutch!"

I bit my lip. In the car beside me, Shawn began to whimper.

Heedless, Terry slammed a glove to the ground and pointed at our house. "Who bought you this house?"

"You did," I whispered.

He flung the other glove down next to the car where our son now sobbed, frightened by his daddy's rage. "Who bought you this car?"

"You did," I whispered again, fighting my own tears.

"That's right, me! Not your God!" He smacked his hands against his thighs. "As long as I have this healthy body and these two strong legs, I'll never need your God!"

He glared at me, snatched up his gloves, and stalked back to the garden plot.

Trembling, I walked around the car, climbed inside, and tried to soothe my son. "Hush, Shawn-baby, it'll be okay, you'll see. Momma loves you."

I covered my face, leaned my forehead against the steering wheel, and begged God to save my husband's soul.

The next night, I stared at the sputtering candles as the special dinner I'd prepared grew cold. I'd found out just that day I was two months pregnant with our second child, and I couldn't wait to tell Terry he was going to be a daddy again.

But my husband was late. Very late.

Finally, the ringing phone shattered the silence. Terry had been in a car accident.

Thankful Shawn was at the neighbor's house, I rushed to the hospital, only to learn that my husband was in surgery. He wasn't expected to live through the night. Thinking of our two little ones, I pleaded with God to spare their daddy.

While I waited for word, I decided I should check on the people who'd been in the other car. With Terry so terribly injured, I knew the other driver must be bad off.

But when I asked the receptionist if I could visit him and his family, she avoided my eyes. "They released him."

I blinked. "Already? Wasn't he hurt?"

She shook her head, still not meeting my eyes.

"Well," I said quietly, "his wife must be so grateful."

She nodded with her lips clamped shut. After a second, she grabbed my hand. "Listen, honey, it's only right for you to know. . . The other driver was drunk as a skunk. He was driving without a license on the wrong side of the road." She squeezed my fingers until they stung. "It's all his fault, and he didn't get so much as a scratch."

She watched me, probably expecting me to throw a fit. I simply nodded and walked away, feeling numb, like I'd been punched until I couldn't feel the punches anymore.

When I got back to the waiting room, I sat in a quiet corner. I told myself that I should be furious, that the drunken fool deserved to be dying in surgery instead of my husband, that no one would blame me for hating him.

But God protected my heart. I focused my remaining

energy on praying for Terry's survival.

In the morning, the doctor came. "Ma'am, your husband survived the night, and we think he'll live."

I burst into tears, and he patted my shoulder.

"I have to warn you, though—" His weary eyes radiated compassion. "Your husband will never walk again. His legs were mangled in the accident, and his feet were crushed. It'll be a long time before he recovers enough even to go home."

Over the next weeks, life delivered one blow after another to my young faith. Only now I wasn't numb to them. My soul felt each and every agonizing jab.

Four days after the accident, I sat down at the kitchen table with our insurance papers and sighed, thankful that at least we had good health coverage.

When I called the company to report Terry's accident and arrange payment for his hospital bills, the representative grew quiet. After a moment, he said, "Ma'am, I'm afraid I have bad news about your account."

I braced my hands against the smooth wooden tabletop. *God, please...* "What do you mean?"

"Our agent came to your house each month for cash payments, is that correct?"

I swallowed hard. "Yes, he told us the rates were better that way."

Silence. Then, "I hate to tell you this, but he was pocketing the cash you gave him. He disappeared two days ago. The police are looking for him." Another silence. "I'm sorry, ma'am, your husband has no coverage with our company. Perhaps he has a policy through his place of employment?"

I hung up without answering. His place of employment? There was no employment now, and I'd stopped working three years before when Shawn was born.

I ran out to the garden and knelt in the dirt. I cradled my hands over the unborn child growing in my womb and wept. *God, are You there? Do You see?*

When I finally cried myself dry, I straightened my spine and started pulling weeds. More than ever, we needed whatever produce I could preserve from this little garden.

Over the next weeks, I developed a routine. I'd spend each long day sitting at my husband's bedside, trying to hide the way my heart hurt as I watched his once-strong body now crushed and racked with pain, wasting away in that white hospital bed.

Each evening, I'd return to the loneliness of an empty house because I'd sent Shawn to stay at my parents' home more than an hour away. Each night, I'd phone my little boy and listen as he begged to come home to me and his daddy. And each time I'd tell him the same thing: "Hush, Shawn-baby, it'll be okay, you'll see. Momma loves you. We'll all be together again soon."

I'd hang up with my little boy's homesick cries still echoing in my heart and run out to the garden, my one place of solace, to tend the plants we so desperately needed. *Is it true, God? Is it going to be okay? Will we be together again soon?*

Then one night a terrible storm swept through. It pounded our poor garden until nothing was left. I was too depressed even to weep. My beaten soul was as barren and hopeless as the little plot Terry and I had worked so hard to make productive. Would we survive?

Seven months after the accident, an ambulance brought Terry home. A body cast covered him from armpits to toes. That night, I gave birth to our second son, Barry.

During the next months, my battered faith was tested beyond all I could imagine. I alone had responsibility for a newborn, a three-year-old, and an atheist in a body cast. Since we owned our home, we didn't qualify for government assistance. My folks gave us what they could, but still I had to juggle bills.

One icy day, I received a shut-off notice from the electric company. I'd heard the government was offering to pay the electric bill for people who needed help if we went to their office, so I bundled up the boys and we went to stand in the long line. An elderly lady in line behind me kept doubling over coughing. She swayed on her feet, and I thought she was going to faint. She told me she was sick, but that she needed this help to keep the heat on.

Finally, when I was next up to enter the office, the lady had a particularly bad coughing fit. My heart tugged. I told her, "You can go ahead of us."

She thanked me and went. When she came out, the government worker came out with her and said, "We're out of funds, folks. I'm sorry."

Feeling like I'd been slapped, I took Shawn's small hand, cradled Barry close, and walked home. *God? This is what I get for trying to show kindness? Don't You care?*

Later that week, after I'd spent our last penny to pay the electric bill, I sat at the kitchen table staring at the empty cabinets. My family needed to eat, and I had no way to feed them. But studying God's Word had taught me He was in charge of all things, so I cried out to Him for help. *You promised to meet our needs, God.*

I prayed a long time until I felt compelled to check my coat pockets. I found twenty dollars. My weary heart filled with praise, and I hurried to the local IGA to buy formula for my baby and food for my husband and son.

I picked up a pound of hamburger, thinking of the chili I planned to make, when the grocer took the meat from my hands. He wrote a much lower price on the package and handed it back to me.

"Thank you," I said and put it in my cart.

The man smiled and picked up another package. He marked it down and handed it to me. Then he did the same with another. And another. And another.

He looked at me. "I have no idea why I just did that."

I smiled. "That's okay. I do." *God, You're amazing.*

* * *

On Easter Sunday morning, my baby toddled around my husband's wheelchair. Terry had graduated from the body cast to leg casts. Still the doctor said he'd never walk.

I was almost ready for church by the time I worked up the courage to ask, "Terry, would you attend Easter services with us?"

He shocked me by saying yes. *Thank You, God.*

We sat in the back of the crowded sanctuary. Terry's wheelchair was parked in the aisle beside my seat. He held one son on his lap while I held the other. The church choir sang "One Day Too Late," a song about an unbelieving husband's grief when his wife and children go to heaven without him. Tears streamed down Terry's face.

After church, he took my hand and said, "That's me, Sherry. You're going to heaven without me because I refused to believe in God." He gestured toward our boys playing on the floor, their bellies full from lunch. "I know now that God's the One who provided all this, not me." He patted his legs—legs that had been casted for nearly two years. "Because I can't."

"But it's not too late for you," I told him. "God spared your life so you could learn that He's God. That He's in control of the universe instead of you."

"But how can He forgive me for what I said? The way I acted?"

So I shared the gospel with my husband that day, and Jesus saved his soul.

Now, thirty-five years later, I climb into the passenger side of the car and smile as my husband closes the door for me. He hobbles around to the driver's side, clutching a cane with one hand and a Bible with the other. He'll never walk without pain, but against the doctor's predictions, he *is* walking. His face shines with a peace and joy that wasn't there before the "accident."

And me? I praise the God of grace every day for being my husband's two strong legs.

A Mother's Heart

We know the excitement of
getting a present—we love to
unwrap it to see what is inside.
So it is with our children.
They are gifts we unwrap for
years as we discover the unique
characters God has made them.

CORNELIUS PLANTINGA JR.

God is the best parent in the world. He knows just how to love us—His kids. And He knows how to discipline, too. (We have a lot to learn from Him, don't we?) If you grew up in a home with awesome parents, you can surely see the parallel between God, our heavenly Father, and your earthly parents. For some, though, there's no way to draw that parallel because the "home" situation was just too painful. The Lord longs to heal you of those past scars and convince you that He's the safest—most loving—Daddy you will ever know. You can trust Him because He's got your best interest at heart—so much so that He gave His very life for you.

Of course there's nothing more amazing for a parent than watching a child grow into a godly young man or woman. What a blessing to see that those years of pouring into him have paid off! And how pleased the Lord must be when we "grow up" into the women of God He longs for us to be. When we give our lives to Him, love others in His name, and seek to follow after Him wholeheartedly, He showers down heavenly kisses upon us. Those XOXO moments abound.

Naturally, He still loves us, even when we're not living right. And if we're paying attention, those hugs and kisses are still ours for the taking. But how it must please Him when we obey! After all, there's nothing better than the affections of a loving, disciplined child. Whether you're a parent, a doting aunt, or the neighborhood granny, you likely know this firsthand.

Does God speak to you through children? Do a little girl's dimples make your heart sing? Does the off-key voice of the boy in the pew behind you make you want to dance? Do you smile when you see a young woman who looks like her mother? If so, sweep them into your arms and tell them. Speak words of encouragement and blessing, not condemnation or criticism.

Just as God has a heart for us—His daughters—we need to have His heart for today's children. They won't be young for long. Before we know, those kids will grow up. They'll be our age. And, likely, they will look at the next generation, wondering these same things we've wondered: "How can they wear their hair like that?" "Why do they listen to that annoying music?" "What in the world is he wearing?"

Yep, the cycle goes on. And on. And on. And God keeps loving His kids, one generation after another. All He asks is that we love them, too.

I thank my God every time I remember you.
In all my prayers for all of you,
I always pray with joy because of your partnership
in the gospel from the first day until now,
being confident of this, that he who began a good work
in you will carry it on to completion until
the day of Christ Jesus.

Philippians 1:3–6 NIV

Almost Friends

By Pauline Hylton

Y ou're breaking up, Sarah. I thought I heard you say
that you want me to go to New Orleans with you." I
missed my street as I spoke to my daughter, cradling the
phone against my ear, tilting my head in order to hear her.

"I did invite you. I talked it over with Crystal and Jenna.
We agreed that we'd like you to come with us. They both
like you. Of course you know that I'm an adult and we won't
change anything that we do when we're with you." She
laughed. "Not that we do anything bad. We're just going to
enjoy ourselves after my graduation. I really think it would
be fun, Mom. You should come."

It was an unexpected compliment. In between her college
graduation from Florida State and her graduate studies,
she'd decided to go "somewhere." And since New Orleans
was only five hours from Tallahassee, with a great hotel

deal, The Big Easy would be their destination. Not only that, but I was invited.

I thought about that for a while. The day in, day out of parenting. The ups and downs of training a child, especially the first—and with no manual. (Not that I would have read it, anyway.)

It started when I found out I was pregnant. My best friend at the time was shocked and not pleased. I think it was because we'd taught inner-city girls together, and she knew that I failed as a mom because I lost my egg.

Not just any egg. In an effort to curb teen pregnancy, we had the girls carry around an egg in a wire basket for a week. No time off, no "eggless" nights. Just caring for and protecting that egg. I flunked. Left my "little one" at a restaurant one night and didn't even miss it until the next day.

My friend was also concerned, since she knew that I wasn't fond of children. Even with her reluctance, my enthusiasm couldn't be squelched. Until I got sick. And fat. And my face broke out. Still, I figured, moms usually liked their children even with the pregnancy malady. With that thought, I endured for nine laborious months.

My mom came to visit and await the arrival of my child. The baby was late. Really late. Mom went home and naturally, the next day I went into labor. There was a problem and I had to have a C-section.

"Come back!" I screamed to my mommy from the operating room as my husband, Tom, held the phone.

She did, and I was glad.

Weighing in at seven pounds, nine ounces, Sarah Ray Hylton entered the world quite dramatically. They wrapped her up in a blanket like an enchilada and tucked in the ends. I couldn't even see her tiny hands. But when they handed her to me, it was love at first sight.

One evening a few years later, we traveled home from church. Sarah was about four, and by then she had a little brother, Micah. He was fastened into a car seat in the back. Sarah sang some made-up song in a clear, sweet voice, viewing the world through innocent, childlike glee. I glanced over at her as I drove. She looked at me with her golden eyes and wispy blond hair. Her simple beauty took my breath away.

I once wrote an article for a magazine titled, "Least Likely to Homeschool," but I tackled it anyway. So when Sarah entered middle school, I was her teacher. Things got tense. They got even worse when she entered high school.

To add to the stress, my parents moved in with us, and my father had to have his right leg amputated.

Sarah attended tenth grade at a public high school. I felt my little girl slipping out of my grasp, but I was so busy with caregiving that I felt as if I were in this dark cave and I couldn't find her. I could barely keep my own footing.

During her junior and senior years, she attended our church school. I worked there in order to help with the cost. Those were long, difficult years. For me, for her, for my parents since dad lost his other leg, too. I didn't enjoy going home, and neither did my little girl.

We barely talked.

Sarah often talked with others. I wondered what she said about me. Plus, I was jealous. I think the root issue was pride, not concern. I needed to grow up.

Life pushed on as she entered a college just up the street. Dad died after her first year, Mom moved into assisted living, and the Hylton family tried to regain some semblance of order and calm. It trickled into our lives like an incoming tide. I had some time to think, and Sarah began to mature. Conversation sprouted again. Barriers were weeded out.

Soon the time came for Sarah to finish her undergraduate degree two hundred miles away. We moved her into a dingy apartment three blocks from campus. Sarah and I worked in the kitchen, while Tom and Micah heaved boxes up the rickety stairs.

"How about we hide your cereal box and dried goods by this door and put a curtain up," I offered as we assessed her postage stamp kitchen.

Sarah was wide-eyed, unsure, yet determined. "That's a good idea."

She unpacked her trendy IKEA dishes and located a low-lying shelf. We continued to stock the kitchen, ignoring the inevitable good-bye. The next day, it arrived. I grabbed my little enchilada, kissed and hugged her, and then I marched resolutely out the door, down the steps, and into my car. I was hysterical before Tom and Micah even made it to the car. They were speechless. The ride home was unusually quiet.

Micah entered his senior year of high school and played football. Tom ran our family business, and I worked from home. I continued to oversee Mom's care and experienced a painful shoulder operation. I knew Sarah was lonely, but I also knew that she was strong. She came home for the holidays. I noticed something different about her.

"You want to get a cup of coffee at Starbucks?"

"You buying?" I asked my second-year Starbucks employee.

"Yep." Neither Sarah nor I needed much convincing to drink the warm brew in the chic store with comfy, retro chairs.

We sat in the corner while fashionable Christmas music played softly in the background. The conversation began on a casual note, then progressed to more serious topics.

After a while, Sarah leaned forward, cradling the warm cup of java in her hands.

"My friend is going through a hard time. She came to me for help. We've talked several times, and I've walked her through some scripture. I've also located some sites online that help with problems like hers." Sarah continued. The story contained heartache, abuse, and even victory.

I sat, stunned. I knew better than to advise. I listened, with rapt attention. I saw traces of my little girl, but she had the fragrance of a young woman. A woman I could like, not just a girl whom I love.

Letting go of our children is tough. It hurts. It goes against everything that is somehow genetically engineered in our being. All those years of teaching, training, failing, and falling met me that day as I stared into that young woman's eyes.

I know that birds kick their young out of the nests, but I suspect it's the male. We, as women, are not made of that stuff. Yet, it has to be done. They can't fly unless they're released to try. Maybe even to fail.

We finished our coffee, but something between us changed that day. Something rough was smoothed. Something wounded was healed.

Last weekend, Tom, Micah, and I traveled to Tallahassee, Florida, to attend my daughter's graduation from Florida State University. Sarah did the mountain of paperwork to transfer there after she received her associate degree here in Clearwater. She found an apartment, and when that didn't meet her needs, she and a new friend decided that they were going to rent a house, and use it for ministry. They found a big, old house with six bedrooms, a handful of baths, and a whole lot of faith.

We picked her up at the house and attended a special reception for the graduates in her department. The next morning we waited with her friends, Crystal and Jenna, while about four hundred people walked across the stage.

It was Sarah's turn. Before she "walked," she lined up on a ramp very near to our seats. I noticed that the graduation cap pressed down on the side of her head, exposing her ear, giving her an impish appearance. She faced us. Pictures of that four-year-old in the front seat many years ago ran through my mind. The small child I dropped off at kindergarten flashed in front of me. The face of a beautiful sixteen-year-old going to homecoming surfaced. The young woman who cradled her coffee and shared with me a part of her life appeared.

Sarah smiled. When she did, her golden eyes disappeared as her smile swallowed everything else on her face. Had there been a mirror, I might have noticed that same all-encompassing smile on my face.

They called her name. Just a name to the announcer, but a lifetime to Tom and me. We automatically "high-fived" each other. Seriously, we did.

That night, we hosted a party at her old house and met more of her friends, and many from her church. There were young men from the Navigator Association, who stood guard in the dining room, eating food as fast as the plates were replenished. There were older couples from church. They play a new part in Sarah's life. Then there was Jeanie. Younger than me, she and her husband, Paul, work with the college students at their church.

Sarah confides in Jeanie. I'm not jealous anymore. In fact, I'm glad. That is what the body of Christ is supposed to do.

After we pried the young men away from the buffet table, and everything was cleaned up, Jeanie and I crashed on the well-used red couch.

Jeanie looked at me. "You know, it takes a village to raise a college student."

"Amen!"

I'm glad Sarah has a village.

Tonight, after I finish this story, I'm going to pack, because tomorrow, I journey to Tallahassee again. Turns out Sarah wants me to attend her grad school orientation. She knows I can't help her. I have zero organizational skills. I think it's my job to just be there.

While I'm there, we'll probably go to Starbucks, at least once. Sarah will speak "Starbuckian" to order a rich delicious cup of java for me, and we'll probably talk. Don't know about what, but it really doesn't matter. We'll be together.

We may stop in and visit her hairdresser, who rumor has it is the best on the planet. We might see the hungry

Navigator guys, and I'm sure we'll connect with Jeanie. Sounds like heaven to me.

I'm going to be prepared. I'm packing some good tunes, my computer, and a couple of books on CD. I'm also bringing a cooler. Homemade banana bread will be carefully wrapped in foil, and Tom caught fresh fish to give to his baby girl, which is one of her favorites. I've got fresh basil and spinach to make pesto. I'll throw in a few other staples because Sarah and I will probably cook together. That is just what we do.

If I know me, I'll forget several items and have to borrow them from some caring soul at Sarah's house.

There is one thing that I won't forget—my egg.

A Child of
the King

You may not be able to leave
your children a great inheritance,
but day by day, you may be
weaving coats for them which
they will wear for all eternity.

THEODORE L. CUYLER

Have you ever considered the idea that you are a child of the King? It's true! That means you're of royal birth. . .a noble lineage. You're a true princess, on the inside, anyway. And God longs to encourage His girls to live lives worthy of one born of royalty. One way He encourages us is by wooing us into His chambers, to spend time with Him. What a privilege, royal daughter! We get to spend one-on-one time with the King of kings and Lord of lords. There, in that secret, quiet place, we can pour out our woes and rest our head against His shoulder. He reaches out with loving hands to take our pain, pressing it into His own heart, and cleansing us from the inside out. Why? Because He's good. Once released from the pain, we can sing praises as never before.

Perhaps you've never been in love. Maybe you don't see yourself as being "beautiful," at least not in earthly terms. The idea of spending one-on-one time with God—or man, for that matter—feels completely foreign. You can't imagine it because your self-image is too marred. When you look in the mirror, you see every spot, every wrinkle.

Oh, if only you could see through spiritual eyes! God finds you to be exquisite. Radiant. He doesn't see flaws or blemishes. He doesn't notice the imperfections. When He looks at you, daughter of God, He sees one who is washed in the blood of Jesus—sanctified, purified, and wholly cleansed. In other words, He only sees His Son.

Today, if you haven't already made peace with God in this area, take time to do so. Perhaps you need to pray the sinner's prayer, and ask Jesus to cleanse you. Accept His work on the cross. Or maybe, if you've already done that, you need to come to terms with the fact that you are God's beloved, His priceless treasure. You are exquisite. Ask the Lord for His vision. For only when you see through His eyes can you truly see "beauty" for what it is.

You might not live in a castle or wear royal robes, but you're born of royalty, just the same. It's time to start living like it! Besides, it's great practice for what's coming in heaven. There, we will live in heavenly mansions and wear honest-to-goodness crowns. Not that we'll keep them on for long, of course. We'll take those jeweled beauties and cast them at Daddy-God's feet, in glorious declaration of our undying love for all He's done in our lives. In the meantime, keep practicing! The King is coming!

And since we are his children, we are his heirs.
In fact, together with Christ we are heirs of God's glory.
But if we are to share his glory,
we must also share his suffering.

Romans 8:17 NLT

No Princesses Here

By Katherine Douglas

"Congratulations! You have a new infant princess!"

The father of Princess Junko (pronounced *June-koh*) looked down on his tiny daughter. He wasn't born of royalty, but his wife was. Between his princess wife and his own important political position, Junko's future held promise. He beamed as she clenched his offered finger.

Here in the Japan of 1936, the new princess had the best before her! Born of royalty, political connection, and wealth, his infant princess would enjoy all the amenities available to one of her station. Junko's proud father could not foresee it, but his family's world would be transformed before she took her first steps—partly due to his choices.

* * *

"We're leaving!" Junko's father declared to his wife a short time later. "You will take my surname. Your father has pushed me too far!"

With that declaration, the lives of Junko and her family were forever altered. Before World War II, a man could take his wife's last name—and often did when marrying into royalty. When Princess Junko's parents cut ties with her mother's family, however, her father dropped the royal surname.

Now under her father's name, Junko's family left the royal ancestral home quietly and respectfully. All ties were severed between Junko's parents and her maternal grandparents. The toddling princess was too young to understand the rift between her grandfather and her father. Her mother did understand, and agreed with her father. Neither Junko nor her mother was ever called "Princess" again.

Junko's father soon left politics, choosing to pursue a successful career in business. Junko remained the daughter of an important man, and she enjoyed a life of privilege. Over the course of the next several years, four brothers and two sisters enlarged their family. Unknown to Junko and her siblings, their father held a key position in the construction and design of a new kind of aircraft: the Japanese Zero.

*　*　*

"Watch me!" Junko shouted. "Watch this!"

Young Junko pushed off down the snow-covered hill, her bamboo skis tied securely to her feet. The homemade skis she and her friends wore gave them hours of winter fun. In the warmer months, Junko learned how to help prepare *mochi*, a tasty rice cake. On Girls' Day in March, pink mochi graced

Japanese tables. White mochi filled up the table on Boys' Day every May. Japan's New Year celebrations meant lots of fireworks and boats decked out with arrays of candles. Junko's earliest school years were fun in her big family. Almost overnight, however, happy traditional holidays came to an end. Japan declared war on the United States in December of 1941.

Food shortages, fire bombings, and strafing runs obliterated carefree days of ice-skating, snow skiing, and springtimes making mochi. A day in 1944 encapsulated Junko's world of the mid-1940s.

"Run! Run for cover!" someone shouted, as the air raid siren screamed its warning.

In a panic, all the schoolchildren ran. Terrorized, Junko ran the wrong way—out in front of the *rat-a-tat-tat* of the warplane's machine gun. The loud drone of the low-flying aircraft, the deafening rapidity of the gunfire, and the puffs of sand around her couldn't make Junko run any faster than her eight-year-old legs allowed.

A sharp pain in her left leg forced a scream of pain from her. Before her legs buckled, a heavy weight from behind knocked her down.

Did the airplane hit me?

Dazed, her heart beating wildly, Junko couldn't move. Injured and breathless, she lay bleeding and trapped. The firing ceased, the warplane's drone faded, but Junko couldn't move. She realized someone—not something—was on top of her, pinning her to the ground.

"Please," she cried. "Please, let me up. I'm hurt."

No response or movement came from the crushing weight upon her. Her leg started throbbing. Bloody scratches on her face and arms stung. She gasped for breath. She heard running footsteps and shouts. With a grunt, a man rolled the unmoving man from Junko. Junko had multiple gunshot wounds in her leg, but the stranger had been riddled with bullets.

He died protecting me.

From that day until the war's end, approaching aircraft sent Junko running for cover. She never learned the stranger's name, but she never forgot him.

Junko's parents never spoke to her or any of her siblings about the bombings of Hiroshima and Nagasaki. As the war began winding down, her father was convinced horrible atrocities at the victors' hands awaited them. He planned accordingly, and one day made an announcement to the family.

"The war is over," he said during their meal one late afternoon. He looked at them, his countenance grave. Junko's skin prickled. "Japan was not victorious. The Americans and others will come here, and we must be ready to do what is best for us."

Junko and her siblings looked at each other.

What did that mean?

"If the occupying Americans ever come here," he continued, "we'll all eat this poison. Together." He hung a small bag of arsenic above their dining table. "It will be better to die together than suffer at their hands."

For three years Junko and her brothers and sisters never sat down to a meal without a furtive glance upward. Junko often wondered, *Will we have to eat it? What will it be like to die of poisoning?*

When her father read in the newspaper that they had nothing to fear from the occupying American forces, he took the poison down and disposed of it. The possibility of a family suicide pact vanished. Yet life for Junko's family changed again—dramatically and painfully.

Junko's father had to relinquish the money he'd made building military warplanes. He and his wife struggled to keep their house and land in post-war Japan. Junko's mother sold priceless traditional family kimonos to feed the family. When Junko graduated from high school, she could not have envisioned what lay ahead.

✳ ✳ ✳

An early morning knock brought twenty-year-old Junko to her door grumbling. With eyes heavy with sleep and her hair in bright pink curlers, she pulled open the door.

"Come swimming!" her best friend invited her. Behind her stood two American GIs.

"What?" Junko demanded. "Do you know what time it is?"

"Time to go swimming! Look at the day! We'll have fun!"

"I don't know," Junko mumbled. "Besides, I can't swim."

"We'll just have fun at the beach. Come *on*," her friend pleaded.

After yanking the pink curlers from her long black hair and grabbing a towel and her swimsuit, Junko was introduced to her blind date. Her friend had been dating the shorter American for some time. He brought his friend, Alan, along for a double date. They thought a day at the beach would be fun. Junko wasn't convinced.

Her English wasn't the best, and this Alan spoke no Japanese. From what she understood, the American flyboy was from someplace in the middle of the United States. He had grown up on a farm and enlisted in the air force right after high school. Junko stifled a yawn. She should have just gone back to bed.

Fun? This guy can't speak a word of Japanese!

He was good-looking and muscular, but Junko found him irritatingly arrogant. She glanced at him again as they arrived at the beach and made their way along the shore. The way he carried himself. . .the way he looked down at her. He towered over her, so he had little choice but to look down.

Just the same, I'm not impressed, she thought.

Junko decided to make the best of the day for her girlfriend's sake. She could put up with this tall American for a few hours. Plus, she could practice her English.

Junko and Alan walked into the water. She made it clear she couldn't swim, but walking in waist-high water seemed safe. She didn't want to drown, even if it meant deliverance from her date.

"Ohhhhhh. . . !"

Junko took a step and went down, down, down into a deep hole. She grabbed Alan by the neck. He had stepped into the same hole, however, and was quickly disappearing beneath the surface, too. The two of them did have something in common, after all. Neither could swim.

Alan grabbed Junko around the waist and threw her up and out of the water toward the shore. With all the savvy and unflappable dignity he could muster, he doggy-paddled his way out of the watery abyss to where Junko stood, blowing water out of her nose, her curly hair now wet and slick as a seal's.

Junko was neither grateful for nor impressed with her inglorious rescue. This. . .*American* had manhandled her and thrown her up to the shoreline like a dead fish! And what kind of man invited someone swimming when he couldn't swim? She decided right then that she and the airman had had their first and last date. . .but, of course, they hadn't.

✳ ✳ ✳

Junko soon learned that, like her, Alan was strong willed and opinionated. He liked a challenge, and found his ninety-pound, pink-curlered blind date as fun as she was challenging. They had gotten off to a bad start, but he didn't give up easily. He persisted, and three months later Junko finally accepted another date with Alan.

By their third date, she decided she liked this headstrong man. A year after their near drowning, Alan proposed.

"I'll talk to your father first, June," he said, using his name for her. "But I want you to think long and hard about this." He took her hand in his. "If he says yes, then I'll propose formally and expect your answer—yes or no. But I've got to tell you something." He hesitated, and Junko held her breath.

What's he going to tell me? Is there some shameful family secret?

"When my military time is done, I'm going back to Ohio. I'm just a poor farm boy, June. I don't have a lot of money, and never will. If you marry me. . ." He forced her to look into his eyes. "If you marry me," he repeated, "you'll probably never see your family—or come home—again. I want you to know that."

Junko nodded her head. She understood better than he knew. She loved him and smiled weakly.

But do I love him enough to leave everything and everyone I know?

Alan's meeting with her father was an all-evening affair just between the two men. Junko's father knew he would likely never see his oldest daughter again if she married the American. Alan knew he would be taking June where she knew no one and where no one he knew spoke her language. He also knew many Americans hated the Japanese people.

"Do you love him?" Junko's father asked her the next day.

Junko didn't hesitate. "Yes, Father. With all my heart."

"He's an honest man," her father said approvingly. He gave Alan his consent.

In 1958 Alan and June spoke their vows before the American ambassador in Tokyo. They spent their first months as newlyweds in Japan and believed getting June's green card to come to the United States would be a simple formality.

When they went to the embassy, they learned otherwise. With McCarthyism rampant in the United States, many Americans feared infiltrating communists. World War II wasn't that far from memory. Were any of June's family communists? Were any of them criminals? Would allowing June on to American soil pose a security risk?

June underwent a thorough and intimidating investigation, but finally her papers were all in order. With the arrival of 1959, she, Alan, and their infant son boarded their first airplane on the long journey to the other side of the world. Once they began flying over the continental United States, anxiety displaced June's excitement.

"We're *still* flying over the US?" she asked Alan after they had already spent hours over United States airspace.

"Yep! It's a big country!" he boasted.

June looked out the aircraft window again.

Does this country have no end? What have I done? Will I ever see another rice paddy? Taste mochi? She held their son tighter.

There are no princesses here.

Hearing and speaking nothing but English every day sometimes threatened to break June's spirit. Homesickness almost swallowed her up like the ocean hole she'd fallen into on the day she met Alan. She longed for Japanese holidays surrounded by her family back home. But she had made her choice.

There's no going back.

Forever
Friendships

When we honestly ask
ourselves which person in our
lives means the most to us,
we often find that it is those who,
instead of giving advice, solutions,
or cures, have chosen rather to share
our pain and touch our wounds
with a warm and tender hand.

HENRI J. M. NOUWEN

Likely you've heard the old song, "To everything turn, turn, turn. . ." Life is all about seasons, and they're constantly turn, turn, turning. Summer quickly passes, and before you know it, red-orange leaves are tumbling from the trees. We've barely had time to settle into autumn before winter's frost makes an appearance. And the snows are heavy upon us one moment, then lifting the next, making way for spring's flowers. On and on they go, these luscious, wonderful seasons, morphing, and then morphing again.

Not that they're all wonderful, of course. Some catch us off guard. They seem to arrive early. We've barely got the Christmas lights hung when a heat wave hits. Or we've just planted our spring garden when a hard freeze sets in. Who can figure it out? And yet, we're called by God to take it all in stride, not to panic. He created those seasons, after all!

Perhaps you've already figured out that our spiritual life tends to run in seasons, too. We go through happy times— bright, warm summers—but they eventually give way to tougher times. We face long, cold winters—say, when a loved one dies or we go through a season of rejection—only to witness the beauty of spring around the next bend. Thankfully, no one season lasts forever.

Never are the seasons more apparent than in our godly friendships. Some friends are meant to stick with us for life. Others are only part of our journey for a brief season. But all friendships are to be treasured. They're a gift from God, who knows that we can't possibly travel this road alone. Sure, there are challenges in every relationship. People don't always get along, and we have to struggle through rough seasons just to see eye to eye at times. But the struggle is nothing compared to the joy we experience as we form lasting bonds. Each friend is a special blessing, even the ones who challenge us!

Which friends are you thankful for today? Stop and offer up a prayer, thanking God for the "heavenly interruption" of friendships. As your friend's arms embrace you, see yourself being cradled by God. That's what He does, you know. . .hugs you through people He puts in your path. (And you thought it was just a simple friendship hug! You didn't realize the King of kings was sweeping you into His arms.)

Friends are here to lift our spirits when we're down, to offer encouragement, and to make us laugh. Primarily, though, they've been placed in our lives to pray. The Bible is clear that the prayers of two or more people are very powerful. So, don't be afraid to share what you're going through with your girlfriends. Ask them to pray. Then watch as God moves through those powerful prayers, restoring broken places in your life.

It's a great season for friendships, sister. . .so dive in!

A friend loves at all times, and is born,
as is a brother, for adversity.

PROVERBS 17:17 AMP

Forever Friends

By Linda Holloway

I stepped from the steamy bathroom. "I'm through with my shower. You can have it," I said to Eloise without making eye contact. I was busy studying my hair in the mirrored closet door. I scrunched wilted clumps. Then I picked at them with my fingers, trying to perk up the too-old-to-curl permanent.

"I already showered while you walked. I'm trying to do something with this hair. It's not long until we need to leave for the keynote session."

Simultaneously we glanced at each other across the hotel room. Eloise sat at the desk in front of her travel mirror, smoothing goop through her black hair. I held both hands above my head and wrapped a dark, damp lock around an extended index finger. We both stared, puzzled at what we saw.

After a few seconds our brains processed unfamiliar beauty tricks. Suddenly we pointed at each other like gunfighters at high noon. . .and burst into laughter. We guffawed so hard, we cried. I backed up to a wall for support and slid to the floor, too weak to stand. Eloise caught her breath first and said, "We're Salt and Pepper all right. And neither of us is satisfied with what we got."

Salt and Pepper—her pet names for us. One short, thin, and white. One short, round, and black. From different worlds. She lived in the "ghetto" as she called it, and I lived in suburbia. She grew up in a single-parent family. My intact family doted on their only child. She experienced Jim Crow prejudice firsthand. As a child, the "white only" signs confused me after Daddy was transferred to the Old South.

Why should Eloise and I ever meet? We worked in the same district but at different schools. I taught disabled students at a special school, and she cooked at a high school. We attended different churches. We didn't move in the same circles. But, one hot Saturday at a prayer rally for our urban district, Connie, our mutual friend, introduced us. It was God's design for Salt and Pepper to pair for life.

The only girlie thing we did together was that ladies' conference. No long lunches. No shopping excursions. No movies. We spent our shared time in prayer, and it bonded us in a special way. Our friendship wove through the tapestry of my life. Its golden thread added rich beauty, both on the image side and the knotty, messy side. Without it my life's fabric would be incomplete.

Three months after the rally, frustrated by the hit-and-miss prayer group we'd joined, I called Eloise. "Would you like to be prayer partners? This group thing isn't working."

"Girl, you're right about that. Connie should be the leader, but she won't lead. This showing up when 'the Spirit moves' is silly. He must not be movin' us at the same time. Or, some of us are ignoring Him."

We decided to meet on Tuesday afternoons in a hospital chapel. It offered a cool, quiet sanctuary after a hard day at school. Two backlit stained-glass windows and dimmed lights completed the peaceful atmosphere. Tension melted from my neck and shoulders every time I entered. So began an eighteen-year journey.

Initially Eloise and I met to pray for our schools. We brought needs of students, coworkers, and administrators. In a short time we expanded our list to cover personal and family needs, our country, and people God brought into our "prayer closet." We experienced interesting encounters in the various places we met.

Ironically, at the chapel we stopped praying aloud when others slipped in to meditate or pray. We didn't want to disturb them and prayed silently for them until they left. One day a young woman dropped into the back pew and sobbed quietly. "We need to go pray with her," Eloise whispered.

We walked to the last row. I touched her arm, and Eloise asked if we could pray for her. She nodded and said, "My little girl is very sick. They are operating now. Please pray for her to survive."

We each prayed aloud. A faint smile brushed her lips after the "amen." Immediately, a young man entered the chapel. "Honey, she's out of surgery. The doctor wants to see us."

She rose to leave. We stood also. She hugged Eloise, then me, and joined her husband. "Isn't it amazing to be used by God?" Eloise said. We never saw the young mother again, but we knew it was important to pray with her at that moment.

Eloise taught me by example about love and patience. For three summers we met at the World War I Memorial at 7 a.m. It offered an expansive view of Kansas City. Many times we leaned against the brick wall and prayed over the metro area. One morning Chris, a handsome young man, approached us and struck up a conversation. His mother was French and his father, African American. He'd lived in the Midwest for two years. Eloise kindly listened as he told us about his life and how he was "doing things I know I shouldn't."

As he droned on, I thought, *He needs to leave. He's interrupting our prayer time. It's our ministry.*

Eloise could read my face as well as my mother did. She nailed me with her piercing brown eyes and said, "It's okay."

I quit squirming and felt reprimanded, not just by her. I realized that this young man's presence was no accident.

He didn't interrupt our ministry; he needed ministry. Even when he asked, not unexpectedly, for money, Eloise gave him a couple of bucks. "Enough to buy a biscuit—not enough to buy booze or drugs," she said, as he walked down the long sidewalk to the park's exit.

Two weeks later Eloise greeted me with her usual hug. "I saw Chris earlier. I believe he's a prostitute. I watched him talk to a man in a big, long car. Then he got in and left with him."

Stunned, I stared at her. I finally closed my dropped jaw and asked, "Before seven in the morning?"

"Sure. Sin doesn't care about time." She crossed her arms across her ample bosom. "We'd better pray for that boy." She reminded me of an ebony Amazon, ready to do battle.

We saw Chris one more time. That morning he waved at us from across the parking lot and walked away. Years later, I still wonder about him and pray.

I learned from Eloise to be ready to listen to and pray with people. I quit teaching to serve in a public office, and Eloise retired. So for six years we met at 7 a.m. in the food court of a high-end shopping area. One morning Carol passed by our table with her coffee and muffin. She smiled toward us. Eloise asked, "Would you like to sit with us?"

She nodded, and we chitchatted for a few minutes. Then a tear escaped her eye. "My son is in prison. He did a terrible thing, and he'll be there for years."

Once again God steered a troubled soul into our day. This time I recognized it as an opportunity, not a nuisance. Love toward this woman flooded me as we prayed for her son. She joined us for five weeks. She gave no indication that she wouldn't be back that last morning, but the season was over. Once again, the end of the story remained a mystery. But we had extended love and prayer while we could.

Each week before our prayer time in that food court we always went to the bakery to get our parking tickets validated. Cindy, the clerk, usually sang out, "Good morning, ladies." If she had time, she limped around the counter and hugged each of us. Occasionally, she asked for prayer.

Most mornings I bought coffee. Sometimes we each bought day-old cookies. My favorites were chocolate walnut. When I handed a package to Cindy, also an African American lady, Eloise said, "Linda loves dark chocolate."

"I know that's right," said Cindy. Her eyes danced as she chuckled and turned to her next customer.

Eloise and I shared mounds of laughter and buckets of tears. We could talk about anything and everything. Our friendship was open and honest. We could express anger, hurt, even childishness because of deep trust.

We prayed each other through deep valleys: her yearlong unexplainable depression, each of my parents' deaths, wayward children, the death of her forty-year-old son, and my highly publicized defeat for reelection to public office.

We celebrated birthdays, little jokes, and notebooks full of answered prayers. We even griped about coworkers and husbands, but only for a short time. One of us would mention Eloise's reminder: "God'll fix it."

After all we'd been through together in sixteen years, her announcement as we returned to our cars startled me: "You know everything has a season. Our season may be coming to an end."

My mind spun. My heart wrenched. I croaked, "Well, maybe someday, but not now—not for a long time."

I sat in my car, started the engine, and wept. *She's wrong. Our season can't be over yet.*

However, within two months diabetes stole enough of her vision to prevent her from driving. Our season of face-to-face meetings ended. Not to be deterred from our mission or our relationship, we talked each Tuesday. We didn't wait for the Spirit to move us, but one of us called at 3 p.m. We continued to share our hearts, but I missed those in-person hugs.

"When it gets warmer, I'll drive over and pick you up. We can go back down to Crown Center to pray," I said.

"We'll see."

We didn't meet, but we continued to pray by phone. The next year Eloise's health deteriorated more. She didn't leave the house except when someone took her to the doctor or the store. She quit attending church. "I'm sure someone would be glad to give you a ride," I said.

"Oh, I don't want to bother anybody."

"Eloise, you helped lots of people over the years. It's your turn."

I knew it wouldn't happen when she said, "We'll see."

In a few months her energetic voice faded. "I'm so tired. My stomach hurts."

"What does the doctor say?"

"He keeps changing my medicine. He doesn't know."

What is this guy? A quack?

Frustration and fear dogged me week after week. I prayed for her health to improve, but she seemed to grow worse. She wouldn't go to another doctor.

I initiated all of our calls and opened with, "How are you today?"

That Tuesday she answered, "I just vomited. I've been vomiting a lot lately. I don't know why."

"Would you like for me to pray quickly so you can rest?"

"I think that'd be best. I'm so tired."

I hung up. Tears burned my eyes. "Oh God, please help her."

I waited to call for two weeks. Eagerly I dialed her number. I was mildly surprised when her husband answered. "Hi, Grif. How are you today?"

"Oh, I'm making it. Eloise is gone."

"Really? When will she be back?"

He moaned, "Linda, we forgot to call you. She passed last week. The funeral was Saturday."

Numbness gripped my body. I couldn't speak. I swallowed hard, but words refused to push past the lump of sorrow in my throat.

Grif said, "I didn't go to the funeral either. I'm so sorry we didn't call you."

I don't remember much of the conversation. I did find out that she refused to go to the hospital and died at home. I babbled something sympathetic and hung up.

I sobbed. I could hardly breathe. I dragged myself into my husband's office. "Eloise died last week."

Jerry rushed to me. I buried my face in his shoulder. "She left and didn't even tell me she was going."

"You know you'll see her again."

I nodded, but tears continued to wash my cheeks. Jerry held me until my quaking subsided. I walked to the kitchen to pour a glass of water. The two roses I'd bought earlier in the day caught my eye. The two-toned beauties made me smile. I took them from the vase, tied together the stems, and hung them upside down to dry. I decided to display them as a memorial to my beloved friend. In time the cream and red flowers dried to a beautiful pink edged with burgundy. They stand in a blue glass vase on my living room mantel, perfect accents to my decor.

I miss Eloise. Her bright smile. Her comfortable bear hugs. Her unconditional love. However, sadness flees when I imagine my arrival in heaven. First I want to see Jesus. Next, Mama and Daddy. Then I'll turn, and Eloise will grab me and say, "Welcome home, girl."

No matter how long I remain in this life, it's a breath compared to eternity. Eloise's exquisite golden thread of friendship will accent my tapestry forever.

Yes, Lord!

What you need to do, is to put your
will over completely into the hands of
your Lord, surrendering to Him the entire
control of it. Say, "Yes, Lord, yes!" to everything,
and trust Him to work in you to will, as to
bring your whole wishes and affections into
conformity with His own sweet, and lovable,
and most lovely will. It is wonderful what
miracles God works in wills that are utterly
surrendered to Him. He turns hard things
into easy and bitter things into sweet.
It is not that He puts easy things in the
place of the hard, but He actually changes
the hard thing into an easy one.

HANNAH WHITALL SMITH

Have you ever made a promise to someone, then neglected to keep it? Or, has someone made a promise to you, perhaps, then weaseled out of it? If so, then you can certainly appreciate the fact that God always keeps His promises. He's not in the business of letting people down. Just the opposite, in fact. If He says it, He's going to do it. Period. Oh, not always in our time—and often not in the way we expect—but He's true to His word, just the same. He can be trusted.

So, why don't we always get what we want in life? Simple. Because our heavenly Father knows what's best for us. He's got our best interest at heart. He wouldn't give us something to bring momentary pleasure, knowing it would destroy us in the end. He loves us too much for that. His will is sovereign, and so is His plan for our lives. He's completely trustworthy, and loaded with great ideas for how to maneuver life's tricky roads. When we have questions, He has answers.

Ironically, we usually run to everyone—and everything—before turning to God. When we're frustrated, we gossip to a friend. When we're hurting, we turn to sugary foods for comfort. When we're down in the dumps, we hide under the covers, unwilling to talk to anyone at all.

So, who do you run to when you have a need? A spouse? A coworker? Your best friend? Sure, they've all got answers. . .and some of them are even good answers. But

God wants to be your first choice, not your last. Sure, it's great when friends or loved ones anticipate your needs and have a ready answer. It lets you know they're paying attention and that they care. They know you, truly know you. And they love you, of course. But *no one* truly knows and loves you like the God of the universe. So, go on. Ask your questions. Just understand that He's already got the answer, even before your question is voiced.

If you've struggled with asking God for something—physical or emotional healing, forgiveness or otherwise—may today be the day you run into His arms. When it comes to healing the pain from your yesterdays, His answer is always "Yes, and amen!" He longs for you to be made whole. If you have any questions about God's promises, you can always read His love-book, the Bible. There you will find hundreds upon hundreds of promises from God to us, His kids. He hasn't changed. He's the same yesterday, today, and forever. So, if He promised it, you can count on it.

For no matter how many promises God has made,
they are "Yes" in Christ. And so through him the
"Amen" is spoken by us to the glory of God.

2 CORINTHIANS 1:20 NIV

The Blessing

By Paula Swan

Justice Boyson looked from the puppy on the examining table to the smiling vet tech who was checking the pet's heart rate.

"She's a beauty. About twelve weeks old, give or take." She transferred the notes from a clipboard to the computer database. Justice watched her long, tapered fingers fly across the computer keys. He noticed the way her glossy red hair swayed with every movement of her head. She was wearing a paw print–patterned scrub shirt and an oversized dog tag on her lapel with the name "Melody" in cursive script.

"What's her name?"

"Harmony," he answered without thinking. The vet tech gave him an attractive smile, and he detected a look of something— was it amusement?—beneath it.

"That's pretty." She turned back to the keyboard, and Justice shook his head to clear it. He had been considering two names for the dog—Sheba and Roxanne. Where had "Harmony" come from? His subconscious? That's what his mother would say.

"The doctor will be in shortly." As she exited through the door that separated the examining room from the surgery, he felt a rush of warm air and heard the yipping of dogs and the soft brush of rubber-soled shoes on the tile floor and a stocky, short man entered the room. They shook hands.

"I'm Doctor Fecik."

"Justice."

"Nice to meet you, Justice." The veterinarian lifted the puppy from the stainless steel table and rubbed her throat gently, whispering endearments into her fuzzy, floppy ears. "Good puppy. Good girl," he murmured, as he gently pulled open her mouth and probed her gums. He ran expert hands over her body. She wriggled and tried to climb into the sleeve of his lab coat. "Looks good. A little on the thin side, but solid as a rock. She'll need her puppy shots and a heartworm test today, and we'll schedule a follow-up visit. Where'd you get her?"

"My porch. She just showed up last week. I posted flyers and put an ad in the paper, but no one came. Any idea what kind of dog she is?"

Dr. Fecik smiled. "A lucky one, by the sounds of it." He looked at the computer screen. "Harmony?"

There was something in the doctor's tone that made his words seem more than just a polite inquiry about a dog's name. Justice felt himself blushing. "It just—came to me—like—like the puppy, I guess."

"Fourth Harmony we've had this year. Last year it was eight.
Two dogs, six cats." He winked at Justice and smiled broadly.
"One was a tom."

"Word association?"

"That's what I figure." Dr. Fecik broke out in merry laughter,
and Justice couldn't help but join in.

"She's a mixed breed. Definitely a little spaniel in there, and
maybe a terrier of some kind. She's feisty." He retrieved the cord of
his stethoscope from between the dog's tiny sharp teeth and gave
her a biscuit from the jar on the counter. "I'll get her started, and
meanwhile Melody can get you set up with everything you need."

"That'd be great!" said Justice. He felt the blush rising again. "I
mean," he amended, "I could. . .sure use the help."

Melody showed him around the retail area of Pet Pavilion
and pointed out the "bare necessities" for owning a puppy. A
tiny leather collar that cost more than his newest necktie, a
matching leash as supple and shiny as butter, and two miniature
stainless steel bowls in a skid-proof rack. He balked at the pink
sweater with a bone appliqué she suggested and chose a petite
Ohio State Buckeyes T-shirt.

"Do you ever take care of sheep here?" Justice asked, as
Melody began scanning items and packing them into brown
monogrammed bags.

"No, we're small animals only, but there's a great large-
animal vet in Port Clinton. Why? Do you run livestock?" She
looked interested.

"No." Justice grinned ruefully. "I feel like I've just been fleeced."

Melody laughed and ran his credit card and gave him a receipt to sign. "You have any other dogs at home?"

"No, this is my first dog. My first pet of any kind. My mother didn't like animals."

"That's too bad."

"Yeah. I always did, though."

"Liked animals?"

"Yeah. Don't know anything about them." He realized that he was still smiling. It had been a long time since he had smiled that much.

"Well if you need anything, you've got my—" He noticed that her cheeks were glowing pink as well. "I mean, the clinic number's on your receipt."

"That's great," he squeaked. He felt himself blushing again and tried lowering his voice. "I mean. . .great for. . .you know. . .for Harmony."

Melody leaned forward over the counter and spoke softly, "The answer is yes."

"Yes? Yes what?" Now he was really perplexed.

"Yes. I'll go out with you. Tonight. At 7:00. I like comedies, and I insist upon buying the popcorn." She continued to look at him with a Cheshire cat grin and dancing bright green eyes. Finally, Justice found his voice.

"Sure—I mean—um—thank you." He realized he was stammering. He didn't often stammer.

"For what?"

He took in a deep breath and let it out slowly, never taking his gaze from her face. "For saying yes." He searched for something else to say and finally hit upon what he supposed was the right thing. "How about dinner first?" He quickly thought about the receipt he had just buttoned into his shirt pocket and added, "A burger or something."

"Sure. Just let me check real quick." She called over her shoulder, "Dad?" Dr. Fecik came through from the examining room with Harmony under one arm and a squirming gray cat under the other.

"Justice has kindly asked me out for a burger and a movie. Mind feeding the kids tonight?"

Justice's heart sank. *Kids?* he thought. *She's got kids?*

Dr. Fecik smiled affably. "A pleasure." He looked at the mountain of bags on the counter and in the cart. "I see she's found a new retail victim. She didn't talk you into anything you didn't need, did she?"

Justice nodded glumly. He was such a dupe. "Probably. But I managed to dodge a few bullets, too."

"The pink sweater with the bone?" Justice nodded. "She's been trying to foist that monstrosity onto unsuspecting fellows for a month." Dr. Fecik fixed Melody with a mock stern look and tried to draw himself up to appear taller, but his daughter towered above him. She kissed him on the top of his half-bald head.

"Diversification, Daddy. It's the name of the game now for small business, and you know our profits have gone up 30 percent since we added the pretty pooch line."

"True." He deposited Harmony in the shopping basket where she curled into a ball of fluff atop the new faux-fleece crate liner and promptly fell asleep. The vet crooned to the cat as he carried it back to surgery.

Justice thought, *I might as well bite the bullet now*. To Melody he said, "You've got kids? How many?" He tried to sound casual, but his voice betrayed him with another squeak.

"Nine—no, ten, I guess. Dad's always bringing home strays. That gray tom you just saw? That's number ten. He was abandoned by the old railroad depot on Saturday."

Justice was so relieved he almost shouted. "Oh! Ten pets—ten—animals! I thought—" he cut himself off, but not before she grasped his meaning. Once again she laughed with contagious merriment.

Melody met him at the Burgers 'n' Things that night, and several other nights that week. She was a wonderful companion. They began to meet earlier so they could linger over their burgers or tacos and talk. By the second week they didn't bother with a movie. They just ate and talked, sitting in the window booth at Burgers 'n' Things or under the willow tree at Petermund Park. Sometimes they met on the porch of the Fecik home, where Dr. Fecik could join them and contribute to the conversation.

They talked about their mothers, and the cancer that had taken them both. They talked about animal care and Melody's scholarship to vet school at Cornell University. She was thrilled with the opportunity—and sorry it would be so far away. She was best friends with her father; Justice's greatest sadness was never having known his. She liked chocolate. He liked vanilla. They spoke of inconsequential trivia and weighty matters with equal ease. This kind of discourse was new for him. He discovered that he had opinions about such diverse subjects as politics, soybeans, and non-chlorine bleach, and no opinion at all about glee clubs, telephone conglomerates, or beet sugar. He wondered how they found so many things to talk about. His own home had been a place of silence and stillness long before his mother had become ill.

There had been few books in the home of his youth, and there were fewer still in his apartment over the store. A yellow phone book dotted with on-hold graffiti, the newest copy of *Sports Illustrated*, a mint-condition leather-bound Bible from his baptism twenty-six years ago, a few how-to books, and the various trade catalogs with which his mailbox was always glutted.

The Fecik home was crammed with reading material. Built-in floor-to-ceiling bookshelves lined the long living room. Books and journals covered every hard surface in the den. Even the bright yellow kitchen boasted a rack of neatly arranged cookbooks on top of the refrigerator.

"Melody," he asked one evening as she washed their drinking glasses and he folded away the Chinese take-out cartons and placed them in the dog-proof garbage pail, "may I borrow one of your books?"

"Of course. Take your pick."

He lifted down a large tome with a dusty red cover. "This one."

She looked at the book and nodded. "That's a good one. Belonged to my mom. She always made the Hawaiian pie." Melody sounded a little wistful when she spoke. She touched the book gently. "See that?" She opened the book and pointed to a grubby

brown mark on the flyleaf. "That's her thumbprint. She put it there day she got the book. Just dipped her thumb in chocolate syrup and printed it." She smiled, and tears welled up in her eyes.

"Why?"

"So she could enjoy the book without worrying about getting the first mark on it."

"Oh." Justice thought he understood. It was like the first ding on a new car. It was inevitable, and one could spend an inordinate amount of time thinking of ways to avoid it, all to no avail. He looked at her warmly and whispered in her ear, "The answer is yes."

With an anticipatory smile she said, "Yes, what?"

"Yes, I will make you the Hawaiian pie."

She laughed and more tears sprang to her eyes. Then, before he knew what was happening, she leaned against his chest. He instinctively wrapped his arms around her and held her as she cried. He wept, too. For Melody. For her mother. For the mother that he would never see again. For every time he had been afraid to let a tear fall, he wept. This, too, was inevitable. Why had he spent so much time keeping grief at arm's length? Long minutes passed and when the sobs had quieted into sniffs, he found the words of the pastor at the funeral coming back to him. "To be absent from the body is to be present with Christ. . . ." He tried to think of the rest.

"To be absent from the body—" he fell silent, as he realized that he had spoken aloud.

"Is to be present with Christ." The words came from the yielding form in his arms. He gently stepped back from her and looked into her now-red and streaming eyes.

"Do you believe that?" he asked.

She nodded. "More than anything. Do you?" She waited, unblinking, as Justice searched for the truth. Finally, he nodded.

"Yes, I do. I had forgotten that I believe that, but I do."

"I'm so happy you remembered," she murmured, as she pressed her wet face against his shoulder. He felt a lump rise in his throat and his voice was unsteady as he answered.

"Me, too." Justice heard a rustling in the hallway, but when he turned around he saw only Harmony, intent upon the destruction of a leather house shoe.

* * *

The next few months sped by. Justice was happier than he ever remembered being. Since the death of his mother three years before, he had been constantly aware of a feeling of heaviness, of loneliness. As manager of the Main Street Hardware Store, he was surrounded by people all day: handymen looking for plumbing supplies, farmers buying gardening implements and barn paint, and young people from the community college dropping in to sign out the lend-a-hammer. And yet the loneliness had lingered—until now.

It was Saturday night. Dr. Fecik had made them a fine spaghetti dinner with crispy garlic rolls and a crunchy green salad harvested that day from Melody's carefully tended garden. They had ended the meal with a perfectly presented Hawaiian pie loaded with fresh pineapple and bananas and topped with coconut cream. How wonderful it felt to sit on the Feciks's stoop in the long shadows of a summer evening, with Melody by his

side and the almost full-grown Harmony at his feet. Dr. Fecik sat on the glider, surrounded by dogs and cats.

For a long time no one felt a need to speak. It was enough to sit in peaceful proximity to one another. The night sounds began. Crickets warmed up their chirping, mosquitoes buzzed, the well pump hummed, the glider clicked respectfully under its burden as the vet slowly rocked. It was Dr. Fecik who broke the silence.

"The answer is yes."

All eyes were fixed on him. The dogs watched him carefully, waiting for the word *treat* to signal their bedtime snack. The cats stretched their slender necks inquiringly, wondering if the vet was finally going to remove himself from *their* glider. Justice and Melody looked at him with amusement, waiting for the punch line. There were rules to this game, and it hadn't taken Justice long to figure them out.

"Yes, what?" he asked, grinning at the vet.

"Yes, you may marry my daughter." Justice's jaw dropped open. "Don't gape at me. I'm sure she'd get around to asking you eventually, but she's going to school in August, and I can't take the suspense all the way to Christmas break."

Dr. Fecik stood up abruptly, and various animals tumbled from his lap. He gave his daughter a warm look and then met Justice's eyes. "To be absent from the body is indeed to be present with Christ. Thank you for reminding me." He hugged his daughter and turned to lay a strong, warm hand on Justice's shoulder. "Good night, son. Receive a father's blessing."

Deep-Rooted
Relationships

Friendship is a treasured gift,
and every time I talk with you I feel
as if I'm getting richer and richer.

Unknown

Remember that wonderful feeling you had as a child when Christmas was coming? You could hardly stand the wait. You stared at the presents under the tree, anticipating the moment you could rip open the wrapping paper. Godly friendships are even more special than that gift under the tree, especially the ones that change your life. In fact, they're more like the tree itself—tall, beautiful, and sturdy.

Perhaps you've heard the expression "deep calls to deep." If you've ever had a special friend—one who knew the needs of your heart before you even voiced them—then you know what a treasure a "deep" friend can be. In many ways, our closest friends are like sturdy oak trees, planted firmly in our hearts. Their roots run far below the surface, latching on and not letting go. And because the roots run so deep, you can be sure the storms of life won't topple them. Even hurricane force winds won't rip them down. True, godly friendships stand the test of time.

Where would you be without your friends? If you're like most women, the answer would be, "up a creek without a paddle." Good friends truly keep us moving when we don't feel like moving. They give us wings to fly, even when we'd rather settle on a tree branch and stay there. They're not just presents under the tree, given to make us feel better. They're lifesavers. Prayer warriors. Soul sisters. We need them, and they need us.

Who else can you depend on to help when you have tough questions: "What should I do with this teenage son who's addicted to drugs?" "How am I ever going to get through this cancer scare?" "What will I do, now that my husband is gone?" "Will I ever find a job, or will I end up living on the street corner?"

Yes, "deep" friends will surely help you carry the load. Because they're faithful, they won't turn and run when the going gets tough. Instead, they will fold you into their embrace and keep you sane. They will cry out to God on your behalf and lift your weary arms when you feel you can't go on. They will give you the courage to put one foot in front of the other.

Yes, deep calls to deep. . .especially in our friendships. Today, take time to praise God for the women He's placed in your life—the ones you depend on. See them as the gifts they're meant to be. Thank God for their sturdiness, their ability to withstand storms—both yours and theirs. Then take a little more time asking Him how you can be a better friend to them, too.

Above all, love each other deeply,
because love covers over a multitude of sins.

1 PETER 4:8 NIV

The Tree

By Shelley R. Lee

Sitting on the porch steps under a pastel summer sunset, I noticed how big one of the trees had gotten.

It took me back to that spring when we had planted it. One of my best friends was going to plant that tree in her yard. How I got it is part of this story.

The first time I met her was at her wedding on a date with my would-be husband, Dave, her husband's cousin. I had never seen such pure and simple beauty, in a person or a ceremony. And if that wasn't captivating enough, they rode off in a horse and buggy on that beautiful day.

She was magnetic and genuine. I soon looked forward to in-law gatherings because I would get to see Kim. With each family gathering, we became better friends. By the time Dave and I were married and had baby Trevor, in Michigan, Dave had gotten a teaching job back home in Ohio where

Kim and Gary lived.

I dreaded the move initially. It meant leaving some very good Christian friends who were instrumental in my renewed faith in God. I was in a spiritually good place in Michigan. I was just sure there would be no Christians in Ohio! Of course the big U of M–Ohio State rivalry goes into play here, but that's an entirely different story. I was incredibly sad to leave Michigan. Home.

Then I thought of Kim, and there was excitement in my heart. Of course the rest is history as they say. And here is where the history is recorded. Kim and Gary were such a blessing to us. I didn't know where to begin with the process of finding a place to live. Kim spearheaded the project. She gathered the local classifieds—the Internet was not even heard of yet—and highlighted several possibilities that might fit. Then the five of us headed out, apartment hunting together. What seemed scary to me at the outset became joyful. She had a way of doing that.

She found us an apartment in the small town of McComb a few miles from their farm, where we would live for the next few years.

Kim grew the most beautiful plants and flowers that this novice gardener had ever seen. "Would you like to take home some peonies?" she would ask me every spring. But the question was really more a formality, being that she was already preparing a moist paper towel in a plastic bag for the freshly cut flowers. They were the biggest, most lush flowers I had seen in my life. I felt like a queen taking them home with me.

As I was loading up kids and flowers to head home from her house one day, I was struck by the rich colorful flowers along the sidewalk. "What are those called?" I asked.

"Moss roses," she said with such satisfaction.

One afternoon Kim invited me over to watch *Somewhere in Time*, a Christopher Reeve movie. In the enchanting film, a photo of his future love interest (played by Jane Seymour) attracts him beyond reason. We learn later that as the photo was taken she was looking lovingly at him. (This occurred in the past but at a later date. . .there was a bit of time travel involved. You must watch the movie!)

It was a fabulous afternoon! We ate delicious frozen pizza bread in her kitchen with a view of her magnolia tree in magnificent full bloom.

One spring Kim and Gary planted hundreds of pine trees to use as Christmas trees in the future. A whole field of trees, and they watered them all. But the tree in my front yard still wasn't planted yet.

Kim also introduced me to *Anne of Green Gables*. So fitting, because she and I were kindred spirits like the girls in the movie. In those years of young womanhood, we encouraged one another in the struggles of making marriage work and raising children well. We grew in our faith, sharpening each other along the way. But I'm jumping ahead in the story.

I can't forget the early years, when I had the only child. We frequently went over on weekends to their peaceful farm and enjoyed bonfires with little Trevor and her beloved bassett hound, Calliope.

One day we went shopping and between stops sat in the parking lot for a long time while she poured out her heart about concern for not being able to get pregnant. By this time I was pregnant with our second child. But Kim was gracious and full of faith; she was willing to accept whatever God gave her.

By late summer that year, we had Hannah and she rejoiced with us. Then grieved with us when she and Gary were the first loved ones to arrive after we found our infant daughter dead one fall morning from SIDS. Kim supported me in great ways that difficult season.

A nurse, she always loved her work. So when she got pregnant, she wondered how she would do balancing work and motherhood. But soon after having Josh she said, "I never knew just how much I would love being a mother." She held him with sweet affection looking straight into his eyes. That year we each had little boys, six months apart.

Less than a couple years later we each had another boy within months of each other—I had Westley, she had Matthew.

Sometime that following year we were sitting on my

porch swing at our little house in Cygnet, Ohio, holding children and watching the older ones play. Kim asked me if I were to have another daughter, if I would not use the name Megan. She wanted a Megan, she told me excitedly.

Sometime in the next year I had my fourth son, Dexter, and she had Megan.

We were done having children, and we each needed bigger homes for them. Within a year of one another we each built homes twenty minutes from one another, in different school districts. Theirs, in a big beautiful wooded lot; ours next to a river and little wooded gully. We helped one another a lot, as we had for many home improvement projects over the years. Dave and Gary did a lot of roofing together. One day Kim and I sat on scaffolding, just the two of us, siding the north side of my house all afternoon. We talked the entire time and got a lot of work done.

But that tree still wasn't planted in my front yard.

After all the hard work we had done, we enjoyed time visiting at one another's homes and letting the kids play while we visited in the moments we had. Kim observed one day, sitting in my floral dining room, how very different our styles were. She was very country; I leaned toward Victorian. She commented on how fun it was that we were different in that way, but enjoyed the beauty of one another's homes very much.

I enjoyed hosting ladies tea parties in those days,

Victorian style, and Kim and her mother, Shirley, attended one of them together on a summer day. I had asked one or two of the husbands to be "butlers" for us, and we all got dressed up. It was such great fun! I was going around getting pictures of everyone. Kim stood in my kitchen, and her eyes lit up as she looked at me as I took the photo. It ended up being the best photo I had seen of her. It was a nice memento of that enjoyable time with good friends.

The flowers were beautifully in bloom, but that tree still wasn't in the ground.

The following spring Kim and Gary and the kids came over, and she made Flubber for all the kids. She had the recipe (that could also be found on what was called the *Internet?*). The kids loved it and laughed so hard at the funny oozing substance. It was a really fun night for all of us.

Still no tree. We're getting there. . . .

A few weeks later I came home from work and found a phone message from a family member. "I'm sorry to tell you this way, but Kim has been life-flighted to the hospital. She has an aneurysm." I collapsed onto my counter in shock, crying and gasping, and then calling my neighbor to ask if she would drive with me to the hospital. I was in no state to drive.

My neighbor, Sarah, led the way. I was in a daze. I could not have asked where ICU was without breaking down. When we got up to her room, they took me in to see her.

I cannot get her intense brown eyes out of my mind. They had immobilized her and given her pain medication. I went right up to her face, and her eyes locked on mine and told me volumes in a single look. She knew me. She had her mind; that was very clear.

I sat with Gary and the family, and the neurological surgeon explained what he would be doing, the risks, and how long recovery might take if things went as planned. We all sat there stunned. *She may never be the same*, I realized.

The next day they took her into surgery, but before she went she asked Gary to videotape her singing "Jesus Loves You" to her children—just in case.

Less than a week later I stood at her graveside on a beautiful grassy hill under a mighty oak tree. Life Flight sent one of their choppers to do a salute during the ceremony. I had never seen a helicopter bow down before. As if I needed something more to weep about. The big church where we came from was packed to standing room only, speaking more volumes about the impact her life had on so many people.

Gary came over with the kids a week or two later. "I have some trees," he said. He and Kim had bought several trees they were going to plant. But now he figured he would share some of them with the people who missed her. He gave us one that looks like a pine but drops its needles in the winter. I obviously never got as good at gardening as Kim was; I don't even know the name of the tree.

Sometime after the tree was planted, Gary called. They were working on her gravestone and wanted a photo of her on it. Her mom, Shirley, loved the photo of Kim that I took at the tea party and asked if I had the negative.

One dream I had of Kim after she died, she was gardening in summer overalls, warm sand beneath her bare feet, in what seemed like my front yard (or maybe I just wanted to believe it was my front yard, but it was my dream). She wouldn't speak, she merely stood there smiling and motioning excitedly for me to come and help her. There was a lot of gardening to be done. I was so sad to wake up from that dream.

On occasion, when I'm troubled, I drive out to that grassy hill under the mighty oak and I see Kim smiling at me, just like in *Somewhere in Time.* That seems like no coincidence to me. It's a gift.

Everything about her was a gift.

As I sat on the porch steps marveling at the tree, I recalled sitting in that very spot several years ago now, mourning and bewildered at the loss of my dear friend, staring at the newly planted tree.

Today it is growing strong and beautiful, just like her.

Today I take life's gardening more seriously. I think about who needs a little seed of hope, who needs a little more sunshine or water. And maybe someday I will be strong and beautiful, like her. Branching out and growing into the wide open spaces, roots deep in what is true, good, and eternal.

Unexpected
Blessings

The will of God for your life is
simply that you submit yourself
to Him each day and say,
"Father, Your will for today is mine.
Your pleasure for today is mine.
Your work for today is mine.
I trust You to be God.
You lead me today and I will follow."

KAY ARTHUR

When you hear the word *submission*, what comes to mind? An angry parent, spanking a naughty toddler until he does what he's told? A ruthless boss, cracking the whip at tired, overworked employees? A spiteful spouse, intent on getting his own way at any cost? There are so many ways twenty-first-century women view this word, and few are good.

The word *submit* doesn't exactly conjure up peaceful images, but it should. For only when we walk in total submission to Christ can we really be set free from the things that bind us. Confusing? You bet! But it might help to know that God's idea of submission is completely different from ours. His version doesn't require cracking the whip; instead, it calls for bending the knee to His will. Accepting the things that seem impossible as possible. Trusting that He's got things under control, even when they seem to be spiraling out of control. Basically, it's God's way of saying, "Take your hands off, honey!"

The Lord asks us to acknowledge that He is God and we are not. He also longs for us to accept His timing, and to walk in the assurance that He knows what's best, even when it appears otherwise. Sure, that means handing over control, but who wants to be the one in charge, after all? Peace—lasting peace—doesn't come from taking the reins in your hands. It comes when we let go and learn to trust that His plan is bigger and better than ours.

So what do we do when things appear to be spiraling? Do we panic, or do we trust? If we're control freaks, we often fly into a panic. Why? Because we don't always see things for what they are as they're happening. Oh, if only we could! Sometimes the news we think is bad—or untimely—turns out to be the greatest blessing of all. Sure, it's hard to submit to God's overarching plan if things appear chaotic. . . if they make no sense in the moment. If only we could see the road ahead as He does! Then we would know that the nonsensical issues of today are most often the blessings of tomorrow!

Let go of the reins, sweet sister. Trust God. He's got you covered—today, tomorrow, and all the days thereafter. Accept life's challenges for what they are: tomorrow's blessings. And don't be afraid to pray: "Thy kingdom come, Thy will be done." After all, God's kingdom—and His will—are simply out of this world!

*May the God of hope fill you with all joy and peace
as you trust in him, so that you may overflow with
hope by the power of the Holy Spirit.*

ROMANS 15:13 NIV

The Honeymoon's Over, Mostly

BY MAURA KLOPFENSTEIN OPRISKO

Everything. I could smell everything. I could smell the tomatoes a room away; I could smell the dust on the TV; I could smell. . .whatever our couch smelled like, and I was valiantly fighting the urge to use the bucket by my head.

I knew Will was tired of this, and I was embarrassed, but completely helpless to stop it. Any minute now, he would come home to find this unshowered, emaciated wife just as he left me this morning. He'd give me a kiss on the forehead, ask me how I was feeling, and then go clean up the cutting board covered in dried-up tomato seeds. Tomatoes were all I could eat. Weird, I know. When I went to cut one up an hour ago, I blacked out in the August sunlight that was relentlessly pouring through the kitchen window, and I caught myself on a chair just in time. So, I found refuge once again on the couch, with my head inches away from the air-conditioner, while the tomato mess dripped everywhere and began to dry.

And he would miss *SG-1* again tonight. There was no way I could get up from the couch ever again. I was sure of it. And, though I might've sucked up my passionate hatred of all things science fiction for an hour so he could watch his one and only show, he was being careful these days. Or something. I'm not sure what it was exactly. Maybe he felt bad for me in my violent illness and didn't want to make me watch something I hated. Maybe he was watching it in our bedroom, relishing the time away from his lump of a wife. I didn't know. But I was a little nervous that he wasn't pleased with this marriage he'd gotten himself into just two months ago.

This wasn't supposed to happen now. He'd moved from Indiana to Cleveland for me. He wasn't crazy about it here, but when he did it, he knew he was about to propose and had my dire job situation in mind. He wanted me to have a chance at finding work once we got married and I moved in. I'd already spent two years living with my parents, just an hour and a half south of Cleveland, and had worked tirelessly trying to find work, to no avail. He knew, at this point, that my only chance was to be in a bigger city, and it made sense for him to be closer to me during our engagement than the six hours we were used to. So, he picked up all his belongings, and set up camp in a city he didn't even like. For me. And then, almost as soon as we came home from our honeymoon and I'd moved in, it was this. It ruined everything.

*   *   *

"Where are you going?" he asked, turning around from the kitchen cabinets, his mouth full of peanuts.

I squeezed my eyes shut. "Oh, come on! You couldn't have waited till the second month of marriage to talk with your mouth full?"

"Nope," he said, smiling widely with peanutty teeth and leaning in for a kiss.

I shoved his face away with my hand, laughing. "Gross, weirdo! I'm going to the drugstore," I said. "I'll be back in a minute. I'm just going to the one on North Park."

" 'Kay," he said, turning back around. And I closed the door behind me.

I let my smile drop. I didn't want him to know—mostly because it was stupid, and it would just freak him out. I'd go get the test, take it in secret, then show him the negative result, and we'd both laugh. He would ask me why in the world I thought I was pregnant, to which I'd say I don't know—I felt funny. Probably just paranoid. We couldn't have a baby right now. Now, I always knew that children were a blessing from God. But it was a blessing I'd rather have gone without until I was thirty. I had too many things to do right now to have kids. I had a career to start. I had college loans to pay down. No, you don't understand—I was twenty-four years old and carried $60,000 worth of debt into my marriage. I had all my belongings to unpack still, for crying out loud. Oh, and we lived in an apartment in a college dormitory. You heard me. Will's job was in residence life, so we actually lived in the dorm. Bottom line: the day we got married, when the inevitable jerk or two made comments on how we would surely come home from our honeymoon with a baby on the way (probably because that's how they did it), we had no time for it. It wasn't funny. We'd respond with a curt, "no," and change the subject. We did *not* want kids. Not for years.

I knew twenty minutes from now I'd be completely relieved. I thought about Will giving me grief about it for years to come. Every time I'd complain about an upset tummy or a very pungent smell from now on, he'd tease me that I was pregnant, and I'd slap his arm. And then, some-day, a long time from now, we'd say, "Hey, let's have a baby."

I stood in front of the selection of tests, not even really knowing why I was doing this. I knew I felt "funny," and really tired. I probably just hadn't had enough protein or something this week, and I'd be mad at myself tomor-row for wasting the twelve bucks. *I'm not even that late,* I thought. *And I have cramps already.* I grabbed the one with the most tests in it, forked over everything in my wallet, and stuffed the paper bag in my purse. As I walked away, the cashier called after me, "Hey, good luck!" I smiled at her weakly, thinking that was the perfect thing to say.

But I never had to wait the two minutes. As long as it took me to administer the test and raise it to my eye level was all the time it took for the little plus sign to show up, but I think I just sat there and stared at it forever. I hadn't considered this. *Pregnant. I'm actually pregnant. Not paranoid. Pregnant.* Becoming parents wasn't "someday" anymore. It was inevitable. It was. . .now.

I stepped out of the bathroom. Then, I chickened out and dove back inside. Deep breath. I reemerged. "Honey?" I called.

He was fussing with our broken fan in the living room, but when he heard the tone of my voice, and saw which room I was leaving, he froze. He knew. I didn't even have to say anything else.

"You're pregnant," he said quietly. There was no question. I nodded, grimacing.

He'd taken a seat on the couch. I sank into the cushion next to him and irreverently tossed the positive test on the coffee table. The rest of the night, we went back and forth between crying devastated tears and sitting frozen in stunned silence.

The cramps didn't go away over the next few days—they got worse. So, I took the remaining tests in the box, thinking that perhaps the first one was a fluke. How great would it be if it were just a bad test? That would solve everything. I could get back to unpacking, salvaging our dorm apartment into some semblance of a home. . .I could get back to my job hunt. But no. Three more tests yielded positive results, and as the hours went by, the pain in my abdomen doubled me over. It was excruciating.

I called Will at work. No answer. I called his cell. Nothing. I called my family doctor two hours away, who told me either to see my OB-GYN or the emergency room immediately. I had no OB-GYN in town yet, so I grabbed a phone book and started with the *A*s. Nobody was nice, nobody was taking new patients, and everyone said to get to the emergency room— *yesterday*. I dialed Will again.

"Where. . .in the. . .*world*. . .have you been?" I snapped, when I heard his unsuspecting voice. "I've been trying to reach you. . . ."

"I was in a meeting! What? What's going on?"

"You need to come home and take me to the hospital. I've never had cramps like this; it's like I—"

"I'll be right there."

Click.

After nine hours in the emergency room, several needle pokes, a painful IV, and another positive pregnancy test (no, really?), we were in the ultrasound room, waiting for the technician to tell us whether or not our baby was being miscarried.

We weren't looking at each other. The room was just heavy with silence, and I thought maybe he was mad at me. Maybe he thought this was my fault, maybe I misinterpreted something a doctor said once about fertile weeks, or maybe I forgot to take my temperature once, or. . .I don't know. But I felt desperate. I wanted so much for him to say something. Or even just look at me, give me a reassuring smile.

I tried to distract myself by calling to mind the million times we were asked today whether or not we'd had a difficult time conceiving. Mostly, we'd looked at them like they had rotten meat on their faces. It would probably be funny someday, but in the moment, I just wanted to tell them to go walk down one of their crazy-twisty hallways and get themselves lost.

My reverie came to an abrupt end when a perky, ponytailed nurse bounded into the room. "Hey, guys!" she exclaimed. Her voice was jarring. It kind of reminded me of being a fifth-grade camper, and waking to the sound of trumpets.

She flipped on the ultrasound machine, got out the scanner, and ran it over my belly, looking for the baby. And then. . .

"There's the start of your baby!" First Trumpet proclaimed, pointing at a white speck. We stared at the screen, dumbstruck. I felt Will's hand on mine.

She spoke up again. "You're not miscarrying," she said. A bunch of air escaped my lips. Relief? Surprised at myself, I looked up at my husband, and there it was. His smile. I grasped his hand back. Hard.

"But I can tell you what's causing you all that pain," she continued. "You have a cyst. A big one, too. Wow, I bet that hurts."

"Is that serious?" Will asked.

"No," she said, "and the baby should be fine, too. The cyst will rupture by itself, and don't worry. . .baby won't mind that either. But it'll probably feel like your muscles are tearing when it happens."

"Awesome," I replied, still studying the little white, flickering speck.

She took a few pictures and printed them out. There in my hands was a picture of our baby. Our *baby*. For the first time, it didn't completely freak me out.

I looked at Will. "We're gonna have a baby, hon."

He hadn't stopped looking at me and smiling. "I know," he said simply and kissed me.

* * *

I thought it was the TV that woke me up, but when I opened my eyes, I saw Will shuffling around in the kitchen. "Honey, I brought you home some penne," he called.

"Thanks," I said. "That sounds good, actually."

He dragged tired feet through the living room and

dropped himself onto the couch next to me, a plastic container and fork in hand. "I thought it might," he said. "Tomatoes, marinara. . .you know." He pointed the fork at me, poised to feed me.

"So what are we watching, here?" he asked.

I bit the penne off the fork and turned around to look at the clock. "Latht week'ph *SG-1* iv on in ten minuteth," I said, turning back toward him, mouth full. His forehead and chin puckered in disgust, so I gave him my biggest marinara smile and flipped to the SyFy channel.

From One
Adventure
to Another

To fall in love with God is
the greatest of all romances;
to seek Him, the greatest adventure;
to find Him, the greatest
human achievement.

SAINT AUGUSTINE

Are you an "idea" person? Do you see life as one great adventure after another? If not, you should! After all, this road we're traveling is loaded with joyous opportunities at every turn. Why, just ahead, up around the bend, a huge blessing is coming! And beyond that—a hurdle to jump. After that, another blessing, and then a ravine. But, never fear! You can make it. Beyond that unexpected gap in the road lies another blessing, then another challenge. . .and so on.

Why, this is better than any African safari! Excitement abounds! There are rivers to cross, jungles to navigate, camouflaged pits to avoid. And can you hear the cries of the monkeys overhead? Their voices blend with the hissing of snakes and the ever-present hum of cicadas to create a cacophony of sounds, all meant to add to the thrill as you progress from one point to another. As you trudge through bogs, clear weeds with a machete, and peer ahead through dust-covered binoculars, you realize the truth: This journey through life might be tough, but it can also be a blast! And talk about an adrenaline rush! Whew!

Viewing life as an adventure can be very freeing. It makes the hard times easier to bear. And this positive viewpoint is godly. He longs for us to journey hand-in-hand with Him, enjoying the moments, even the tough ones. So, why worry? With God's hand in yours—and life as a grand adventure— even the negatives can be turned to positives. How, you ask?

Through prayer and daily submission to His will.

Lest you think you're alone on this trek. . .the adventurous God-follower is in good company. Search the scriptures and you will find dozens of examples of men and women who, just like you, chose to trust God with their wants and wishes. And He led many of them on the adventure of a lifetime. Some—like Elijah—soared to the highest heights. Others—like Joseph—were plucked from the lowest depths. Still others witnessed mighty miracles—water turning into wine and people being raised from the dead! Wow!

Be careful, though! This adventurous trek might take you to some unforeseen places. Who knows! You might just end up walking on water. Or dashing through a parted sea. Or eating heavenly manna. You never know, when your tour guide is the King of kings and Lord of lords! He has a way of surprising you! (And what adventurer doesn't love a few surprises as she journeys along?)

Yes, you're in great company. And isn't it encouraging to know that others have walked this road before you? They've paved the way, their faith strong, their feet sure. If they can do it, you can, too.

*"Don't worry about anything; instead, pray about everything.
Tell God what you need, and thank him for all he has done."*

Philippians 4:6 NLT

What a Great Idea!

By Kathy Douglas

My husband and I are ideally suited, but not because he's my Ideal Man. Idealism wilts like old lettuce when one marries not the Ideal Man, but an *Idea* Man. This is my story, and I'm not making up a word of it.

Some women claim they married the Right Man. Others moan they married the Wrong Man. Still others admit to having married the Boy Next Door or their High School Sweetheart. Some might boast that they did, in fact, marry the Ideal Man. (Those who make that boast include women who have been married for less than fifty minutes or for more than fifty years.) For those of us who have married Idea Men instead of Ideal Men, one letter does not the only difference make.

My first whispered warning that my Ideal Man was an Idea Man came the third time I saw him extract a large wad of cash from his pocket to pay for our date. My Idea Man's sense of humor was what initially captured my heart—not his money. He won me over making me laugh. To this day my heart wears a smiley face most of the time.

When he pulled out a fistful of bills on that memorable third date, however, I decided, *Bonus! This guy is flush with cash!* Our courtship held promise independent of money, but this unexpected display of wealth got me thinking. *Maybe I can be a stay-at-home wife and mother. Wouldn't that be great?* Not suspecting my own self-delusion, I smiled to myself. *He* is *ideal!*

Cash, I learned as our love and relationship progressed, was how this man paid for almost everything. That's why he had so much on hand. His idea? The smart guy pays as he goes with no middleman to muck things up.

When we began dating over thirty years ago, credit cards were just starting to wheedle their indispensable presence into the American wallet. Internet banking was the stuff of sci-fi enthusiasts. Back then everyone—everyone—myself included, had a checking account. As archaic as that sounds now, that was how most of us paid for utilities, rent, and dates. Not my Idea Man.

Cash or a cashier's check was his modus operandi. He didn't like banks. He didn't trust banks. He still doesn't. His idea, since the time he could spell the word *bank*, is that banks can't be trusted with anyone's money but their own. That should have alerted me that life married to an Idea Man, even if he were my ideal, would be somewhat atypical. My Idea Guy, like all Idea Men, lives in a different reality than the rest of us.

Not only do Idea Men think differently than the rest of us, they do things differently than most of us, too. My Idea Guy did things his way. Call an appliance repairman for a failing refrigerator? Call a plumber for a leaky faucet? Get the name of a good mechanic to tinker with the car? No way!

His idea was to always try his hand at a project first. He tackled problems or projects on his own. I grew more convinced that he was my Ideal Man: thrifty, smart, independent, industrious. I was impressed—and smitten.

When we spoke our vows, I stood assured the gentleman beside me was my Ideal Man. Frankly, I still didn't get it. I was marrying, first and foremost, an Idea Man. Soon my newlywed idealism lay mangled under the advancing parade of my husband's new or better ideas. I began to realize I had snuggled in with an Idea Man for life.

One day my Idea Man announced we should move to the country. Why someone used to the convenience of city living desired relocation to country *inconvenience* mystified our friends. I was somewhat mystified myself, but the Idea Guy assured me this was a great idea.

"Let the naysayers be hanged," he said. "We're moving out!"

Construction of a new home, I soon learned, fans an Idea Man's creative spark into wildfire. In keeping with his idea-ism, my Idea Guy did most of the work. Electrical, plumbing, central vacuuming—what he tackled was as impressive as the finished product. He amazed me along every step of the way—just like he had before we were married. My love and admiration deepened for my mate, this near genius. I allowed myself to relax about his big idea, our move to the country.

We started moving items from our city house to our new country home. A few small doubts tried to worm their way into my subconscious, but I squelched them. This was his best idea yet, I told myself. A few glitches along the way provided me with some tense moments, however, and I upped my intake of antacids. Example: the clothes dryer move.

Some of life's riskiest ideas come to Idea Guys when they're home alone. My Idea Man decided he could single-handedly move our clothes dryer up sixteen basement steps with a little rope, a bit of muscle, and a lot of ingenuity. Then he would pop it into the back of his truck and deliver it to the new house.

Mr. Idea was marginally successful at first. All by himself, and with his own mental grit and brute strength, he got the dryer up to step number fourteen.

Bang. . .thump. . .bang. . .thump. . .bang. . .thump. . .

He stood there with the rope limp in his hands. The clothes dryer was back in the basement. . .not exactly upright, and not exactly in the same condition as it was on step number fourteen. Later he said it was like watching the dryer rappel down the steps in slow motion. He stopped to rethink his failed idea.

* * *

Idea Men don't quickly surrender to the possibility that some ideas aren't necessarily *good* ideas. His mind whirled as he stood at the top of the stairs, looking down on the dented dryer below.

What do I have to lose? The thing has already tumbled down fourteen steps. It doesn't look too bad.

After a few mental recalculations, he practically skipped back down the basement stairs. He wrapped the rope around the dented dryer at a different angle. Exhaling a loud grunt, he restarted his dryer hoist up the steps for round two.

"Voilà!" he declared when the dryer stood next to him on the landing. He got the still functional, slightly dented dryer out to the new house without another problem. Proof positive that Idea Men are as persistent as they are creative.

As we migrated to the country, I recalled the earliest biblical contrast between city and country living. God commanded Noah and his family to scatter and "fill the earth" (Genesis 9:1). When men decided some years later to build themselves a city so that they "*not* be scattered over the face of the earth" (Genesis 11:4), the results were disastrous. It's safe to say country living is God's better idea.

After that brief biblical reflection, my logical conclusion followed: my Idea Man wasn't far wrong (if at all) to move us out of the city, even if the dryer did get a bit banged up in the process. That said, our move opened the gate for more ideas to flourish like the hybrid corn encircling us.

One night we sat curled up together, listening to myriads of crickets rub their legs together in a cacophony of country-style music. My Idea Man planted a tender kiss on my forehead, and told me he had always harbored a secret desire. I raised a wary eyebrow.

"Oh?"

"I've always wanted to fly. Alone. We've got enough space for a hangar, enough land for an airstrip, and enough money to be financially creative. Why not?" he asked.

Before I could organize my thoughts into some kind of rational response, the Idea Man flew into action. The cricket concert forgotten, he went out and bought a kit to build his own airplane. Why—so went his thinking—get aboard a cramped and crowded plane with a bunch of other cramped and crowded passengers when you can build and fly your own aircraft in comfort and privacy?

He had never done this before. Nor had he ever taken flying lessons. He had no degree in aeronautical engineering, and had probably never seen the inside of a hangar. Unlike his wife, he wasn't a *Star Trek* buff. But he had this idea that he could build a plane and fly it. He would build the ultralight aircraft first, and take the flying lessons second. Such a simple, yet marvelous idea.

He built the aircraft, naming her *Harriet Mable* after his mother. I'm not sure his mother was particularly flattered, but the name was emblazoned in bright blue on the canary yellow airplane. *Harriet* (the aircraft, not my mother-in-law) taxied well under the command of the Idea Man on our grassy airstrip once he got her built.

When the time came, she flew well, too—with the Idea Man's flight instructor at the controls. The test pilot's words, after *Harriet*'s maiden flight, went something like this. . .

"You'll never get her up on your own," stated the seasoned pilot. My Idea Guy stood there grinning like a schoolboy. He had watched his creation take to the skies like a fledgling winging its way above the treetops.

"Nope," the flight instructor continued, "I didn't think I'd ever get her airborne. Too much plane, too little engine."

My Idea Man remained undaunted. He confided in me later, "*Harriet Mable flew*. That's the important thing."

Well, yes, he was right there. She did fly. After bumping and grinding across—not one but *two*—large, mowed fields and barely clearing the electrical wires strung along the road.

Wisely, my Idea Guy decided he should release his plywood and polyester pigeon to the bidding of an experienced pilot. Besides, he had begun to learn—with my gentle reminders—that this whole flying adventure had become one big money pit. Idea Men never lack for more ideas. Money, maybe, but not ideas. So my Idea Guy sold *Harriet Mable* (the aircraft, not his mother). He came up with a new idea: build a windmill.

I repeat, I am not making up any of this.

Power loss during inclement weather stalks us country folk like a barn cat on the trail of an unsuspecting mouse. In a burst of genius, the Idea Man decided having our own power source would be a good idea. Maybe even a great idea.

"Why don't you just go out and buy a standard gasoline generator like most people do?" I asked foolishly. Wives of Idea Men do well not to ask those kinds of questions. The answers are convoluted and, in their own scary way, quite convincing.

Once the windmill dominated the northeast corner of our house, the huge, wind-powered, aerodynamic blades did us proud. My Idea Guy beamed with unbridled gratification when total strangers stopped their cars and asked with awe, "Is that a wind generator?" Such awe and admiration is very empowering to an Idea Man.

As it turned out, the wind generator wasn't a bad idea at all. An expensive one, but not a bad one. Time passed, however, and property taxes increased (the latter invariably follows the former). The Idea Guy decided to downsize. He didn't need the landing strip or hangar anymore, so it wasn't a hard decision to make. He disassembled the windmill and packed it up for our final move.

Just when I had begun to think my Idea Guy might no longer pursue any more unusual ideas, he surprised me yet again. Weeks before my birthday, he started to get almost giddy.

"I got you the perfect birthday present," he confided. He couldn't contain his glee, so convinced was he that he had outdone himself. This, he told me, was probably his greatest idea ever.

My birthday arrived. With trembling hands, he handed me my gift.

"Here it is," he said, "the mother of all birthday gifts." He was serious, excited, and clearly proud. "Open it!" His eyes danced with anticipation.

I did. Stupefied, I looked down. I looked up.

"Well?"

I looked down again. Words failed me as I beheld the sight: the mother of all birthday gifts. His greatest idea ever.

My first handgun.

Me, who had never touched a gun in her life.

"We can go target shooting together!" he crowed.

Such has been the pattern of my thirty-plus years of life with an Idea Man. Sometimes it's been frightening. Like the time we almost had a northern Ohio prairie fire when he put a match to some dried grass and weeds. Sometimes it's been great fun, providing hours of entertaining videos. Like the time he almost drove the *Harriet Mable* into our living room. But those are stories for another time.

Yes, the guy whose name I took is more Idea than Ideal Man. Our story ends happily ever after. The last time I checked—after all these years of handmade aircraft and windmills and mind-boggling birthday gifts—we *still* don't have a bank account.

Dear Lord, how can I begin to thank You for the many ways You pour into my life? When I'm down, You send friends to cheer me up. When I doubt my parenting skills, my child or spouse whispers a "well done" in my ear. When I feel I'm overwhelmed with life, You offer heavenly XOXOs—Your surprise hugs and kisses. May my eyes ever be opened to the many ways You're moving in and through me from day to day, season to season. I don't want to miss a thing, Lord. Thank You, from the bottom of my heart.

A Final Thought: It's All about Attitude

Life is all about attitude, isn't it? And it's easy to have a great attitude when you realize that God is in control. He's got everything covered. He wants us to let go and allow Him to work. Today, make up your mind to give Him every facet of your life—your wants, wishes, dreams. Your children, spouse, job. . .all of it. Only in giving it all up can He truly move.

If you're struggling through a season of grief, give that to Him, as well. There's no greater healing than a Christ-centered one. The Lord can sift through the pain and pluck out the good. Be on the lookout for heavenly hugs and kisses as you move from wounded to winner. Why? Because you're a child of the King. You're born of royalty. And the King adores you!

Remember, God is only a prayer away, ready to comfort and heal. His very presence envelops us, even when we feel alone. Best of all, He offers courage when we have none, and patience to see us through the rough patches. Just one more benefit to being born of royalty.

So what are you waiting for, daughter of God? Run into His arms. Spend time with Him. Then, as you head back to your everyday life, keep your eyes wide open. There are going to be heavenly surprises around every bend. . .if you're watching!

Contributors

Amy Blake is a pastor's wife and homeschooling mother of four from Columbus, Ohio. She holds a BA and MA in English from Mississippi College. She has written short stories and articles for *Focus on the Family*, *Mature Years*, *Significant Living*, and *Partners*. She contributed to Barbour's *Book Lovers' Devotional*. Amy won four awards at St. David's Christian Writers Conference, 2009. She has completed two of a projected five *Levi Prince* young adult fantasy novels.

Kathy Douglas enjoys leading women's Bible studies at her church, spoiling her four grandsons, in-line skating—and (rarely) target shooting when she's not laughing at her husband's antics or running scared from his newest idea. You can read her blog at www.katherine-kathy-douglas. blogspot.com or find a listing of all her books on her website, www.katherinedouglas.com.

Linda Holloway is a freelance writer, teacher, and speaker who lives in Prairie Village, Kansas, with Jerry, her husband and best friend. She worked as an educator for thirty-plus years, most of them teaching students with special needs. She now teaches adult creative writing classes and speaks at women's ministry events. God has blessed her with many sweet friendships throughout her life—coffee, chocolate, and conversation with a lady pal. . .lovely.

Pauline Hylton writes from Clearwater, Florida. She lives with her husband, almost-grown son, ninety-year-old mother, and not-too-bright dog. She specializes in humor, or whatever else you pay her for. Currently, she is finishing the last chapter of her book titled *A Caregiver's Walk*. Pauline is fifty-ish (none of your business about the "ish" part) and enjoys teaching God's Word to women. She loves the Lord, her family, and dark chocolate—not necessarily in that order.

Shelley R. Lee is a freelance writer who has authored two books, numerous articles, and recently contributed to *Heavenly Humor for the Dog Lover's Soul* (Barbour Publishing). She grew up in Michigan and earned her bachelor's degree at Grand Valley State University where she met her husband, Dave, who she originally thought was. . . a jerk. They reside in rural northwest Ohio with their four teen- and college-age sons and never enough groceries. She posts humorous stories regularly at www.shelleyrlee. blogspot.com.

Maura Klopfenstein Oprisko is a freelance writer living in Crawfordsville, Indiana, with her amazing husband and two wonderful children. She has a BA in professional writing from Taylor University and is planning to get her master's in journalism and psychology. She aspires toward becoming a mental health journalist.

Valorie Quesenberry is a pastor's wife, mother of four, blogger, speaker, and writer. She is the author of two books, *Reflecting Beauty: Embracing the Creator's Design* (Wesleyan Publishing House, 2010) and *Redeeming Romance: Delighting in God's Love* (to release in 2011). Valorie enjoys communicating truth through both fiction and nonfiction.

Paula Swan inherited a love for reading from her grandfather, Chester Arthur Smith. She has an AA in world languages and a BA in children's book development. Paula lives in Toledo, Ohio, with her husband, Craig, their exchange student, JinWoong Kim, and their rat terriers, Jot and Tilly. Her recent publications include contributions to *Pathways* and *Compass Points* journals and *Heavenly Humor for the Dog Lover's Soul,* also from Barbour Publishing. Paula's email is: pswan@theuglyducklings.net.

Martha Willey is married and has three sons. Her interests include writing, reading, and needlework. She works as a paraprofessional in an elementary school with students who have special needs. Martha has been published in numerous magazines, as well as Barbour's *Daily Comfort for Caregivers* and *The 365-Day Fun Bible Fact Book.*